Level 1, Part 2

Integrated Chinese

中文聽說讀寫

Traditional Character Edition
Workbook

Tao-chung Yao and Yuehua Liu
Yea-fen Chen, Liangyan Ge and Xiaojun Wang

Cheng & Tsui Company

First edition

Cheng & Tsui Company
25 West Street
Boston, MA 02111-1268 USA

Traditional Character Edition
ISBN 0-88727-270-3

Companion textbooks, character workbooks and audio tapes are also available from the publisher.

Printed in the United States of America

PREFACE

In designing *Integrated Chinese, Level One* workbook exercises, we strove to give equal emphasis to the students' listening, speaking, reading, and writing skills. There are different difficulty levels in order to provide variety and flexibility to suit different curriculum needs. Teachers should assign the exercises at their discretion; they should not feel pressured into using all of them and should feel free to use them out of sequence, if appropriate. Moreover, teachers can complement this workbook with their own exercises.

I. *Listening Comprehension*

All too often listening comprehension is sacrificed in a formal classroom setting because of time constraint. Students tend to focus their time and energies on the mastery of a few grammar points. This workbook tries to remedy this imbalance by including a substantial number of listening comprehension exercises.

There are two categories of listening exercises; both can be done on the students' own time or in the classroom. In either case, it is important to have the instructor review the students' answers for accuracy.

The first category of listening exercises consists of a tape recording of each lesson. For the exercises to be meaningful, students should *first* study the vocabulary list, *then* listen to the recordings *before* attempting to read the texts. The questions are provided to help students' aural understanding of the texts and to test their reading comprehension.

The second category of listening exercises consists of a tape recording of three or more mini-dialogues or solo narrations. These exercises are designed to recycle the vocabulary and grammar points introduced in the new lesson. Some of the exercises are significantly more difficult since students are asked to choose among several possible answers. These exercises, therefore, should be assigned towards the end of a lesson, when the students have become more familiar with the contents of the texts.

II. *Speaking Exercises*

Here, too, there are two types of exercises. However, they are designed for different levels of proficiency within each lesson and should be assigned at the appropriate time. In the first type, to help students apply their newly-acquired vocabulary and grammatical understanding to meaningful communication, we ask concrete, personal questions related to their daily lives. These questions require a one or two-sentence answer. By stringing together short questions and answers, students can construct their own mini-dialogues, practice in pairs or take turns asking or answering the questions.

Once they have gained confidence, students can progress to more difficult questions where they are invited to express opinions on a number of topics. Typically, these questions are abstract, so the students will gradually learn to express their opinions and give their answers in paragraph-length discourse. As the school year progresses, these types of questions should take up more class discussion time. Because this second type of speaking exercise is quite challenging, it should be attempted only *after* students are well-grounded in the grammar and vocabulary of a particular lesson. This is usually *not immediately* after completing the first part of the speaking exercises.

III. Reading Comprehension

There are three to four passages for reading comprehension in each lesson. The first passage--usually short and related to the lesson at hand--recycles vocabulary and grammar points.

The second passage consists of slightly modified authentic materials, such as print advertisements, announcements, school diplomas, newspaper articles, etc. This passage may contain some unfamiliar vocabulary. The purpose of these materials is to train students to scan for useful information and not to let the appearance of a few new words distract them from comprehending the "big picture." Here, the teacher has a particularly important role to play in easing the students' anxiety about unfamiliar vocabulary. Teachers should encourage the student to ask: What do I really need to look for in a job announcement, a personal ad, or movie listings? Students should refer frequently to the questions to help them decipher these materials and should resist looking up every new word in their dictionary.

IV. Writing and Grammar Exercises

A. Grammar and Usage

These drills and exercises are designed to solidify the students' grasp of important grammar points. Through brief exchanges, students answer questions using specific grammatical forms or are given sentences to complete. By providing context for their exercises, students gain a clearer understanding of the grammar points and will not treat them as simple, mechanical repetition drills.

Towards the last quarter of the lessons, students are introduced to increasingly sophisticated and abstract vocabulary. Corresponding exercises help them to grasp the nuances of new words. For example, synonyms are a source of great difficulty, so exercises are provided to help students distinguish between them.

B. Translation

Translation has been a tool for language teaching throughout the ages, and positive student feedback confirms our belief that it continues to play an important role. The exercises we have devised serve to reinforce two primary areas: one, to get students to apply specific grammatical structures; two, to allow students to build on their ever-increasing vocabulary. Ultimately, our hope is that this dual-pronged approach will enable students to understand that it takes more than just literal translation to convey an idea in a foreign language.

C. Composition

This is the culmination of the written exercises and is where students learn to express themselves in writing. Many of the topics overlap with those used in oral practice. We expect that students will find it easier to put in writing what they have already learned to express orally.

TABLE OF CONTENTS

Lesson Twelve   Dining

I. Listening Comprehension

Section One (Listen to the tape for the textbook) (True/False)

A. Dialogue I
(   ) 1. There are no seats left in the restaurant.
(   ) 2. The woman doesn't eat meat, but the man does.
(   ) 3. They both ordered hot and sour soup.
(   ) 4. They both ordered cola.
(   ) 5. They decided not to order the tofu dish because it has meat in it.
(   ) 6. They requested fast service because they were in a hurry.

B. Dialogue II
(   ) 1. The dining-room serves Chinese food only.
(   ) 2. The sweet-and-sour fish is sold out.
(   ) 3. The student ordered a cucumber salad dish in addition to the fish dish.
(   ) 4. The student spent more than fifteen dollars on the lunch.
(   ) 5. The dining-room staff member recommended cucumber salad because it tastes very good.
(   ) 6. The dining-room staff member discovered that the student paid him one dollar too much.

Section Two (Listen to the tape for the workbook)

A. Narrative (True/False)

(   ) 1. Wang Peng likes dumplings the best in the Chinese restaurant.
(   ) 2. Wang Peng arrived in the States two months ago.
(   ) 3. Wang Peng is not used to American food.
(   ) 4. Wang Peng is a good cook.
(   ) 5. Wang Peng likes the hot-and-sour soup in the restaurant very much.

B. Dialogue I (Multiple choice)

(   ) 1. Why did the man not drink any beer?
     a. He had to drive.
     b. He had to go to class.
     c. He had drunk too much beer already.

(   ) 2. What did he finally get from the woman?
     a. A bottle of coke.
     b. A glass of coke.
     c. A can of coke.

C. Dialogue II (Multiple choice)

(   ) 1. What is the relationship between the man and the woman?
      a. Husband/wife   b. Customer/waitress
      c. Father/daughter   d. Brother/sister

(   ) 2. Which of the following was NOT mentioned in the conversation?
      a. tofu   b. soup   c. beer   d. rice

(   ) 3. What did the man order for his meal?
      a. A tofu dish, a fish dish, and a soup
      b. A fish dish, a soup, and rice
      c. A fish dish, a beef dish, and a soup
      d. A tofu dish, a soup, and rice

II. Speaking Exercises

Section One (Answer the questions in Chinese based on the dialogues)

A. Dialogue I
1. How did the waiter greet the customers when they entered the restaurant?
2. Did the customers order any meat dishes? Why?
3. Please name all the food items they ordered in the restaurant?
4. Did they order any drinks? Why did the woman ask the waiter to rush?

B. Dialogue II
1. What did the dining-room staff member say about the fish dish?
2. What was the reason for the dining-room staff member to recommend the cucumber dish?
3. Please give the price for each of the food items that the student ordered.
4. What did the student say after receiving the changes?

Section two
A. You and your friends are in a Chinese restaurant. You like different kinds of food. So you discuss with the waiter about what to order. It turns out that everyone enjoys the food. Each student may play a role.

B. After the dinner, you and your friends discuss how to pay the bill. When the bill comes, you find that the waiter has over-charged you one dollar. You talk to the waiter about it.

III. Reading Comprehension

Section One

A. Answer the following questions about the dialogues.

Dialogue I

1. 誰吃素？

2. 他們點了些什麼菜？

3. 王先生喝的東西跟李小姐喝的東西一樣嗎？他們喝什麼？

4. 你覺得他們餓嗎？為什麼？

Dialogue II

1. 這個學生今天晚上想吃中餐還是西餐？

2. 他點了哪兩個菜？

3. 一兩米飯多少錢？

4. 學生給了師傅多少錢？

5. 師傅多給了學生多少錢？

B. Read the passage and answer the questions. (True/False)

今天中午老張請老王到餐館吃飯。老張要老王點菜，老王不吃肉，所以點了一個家常豆腐，還點了一個涼拌黃瓜。這些菜很便宜。老張不知道老王不吃肉，所以點了一盤牛肉，還有一盤糖醋魚。這些菜都很貴。菜上來了，老張想讓老王吃貴的菜，所以他吃了很多豆腐和黃瓜。吃完飯以後，盤子裏還有很多魚和牛肉，可是老王還覺得很餓。

(　) 1. 今天的午飯是老王請客。
(　) 2. 老張和老王一共點了四個菜。
(　) 3. 老張點的菜很便宜。
(　) 4. 吃午飯的時候，老張才知道老王不吃肉。
(　) 5. 老張吃了很多豆腐和黃瓜，因為他也不喜歡吃肉。
(　) 6. 吃飯以後，盤子裏還有很多豆腐和黃瓜。
(　) 7. 老王沒有吃牛肉和魚。

C. Read the following and answer the questions. (Multiple choice)

美味快餐店

菜		湯	
1. 宮保雞丁	$5.95	1. 蛋花湯	$2.95
2. 紅燒牛肉	$6.50	2. 酸辣湯	$2.95
3. 炒魚片	$6.50	3. 雞絲湯	$2.50
4. 京都排骨	$4.95	4. 豆腐湯	$1.50
5. 家常豆腐	$3.95		

(　) 1. This restaurant provides _____.
   a. buffet   b. banquet   c. fast food   d. free delivery

(　) 2. 要是你只有五塊五毛錢，你想吃一菜一湯，你可以點_____。
   a. 炒魚片、豆腐湯   b. 家常豆腐、雞絲湯
   c. 京都排骨、蛋花湯   d. 家常豆腐、豆腐湯

D. Read the note below and answer the questions. (True/False)

小王：

　　　小張剛才給你打電話，想請你跟你太太這個星期六去他們家吃餃子。他現在在他的辦公室。請你回來以後，給他打個電話。

　　　　　　　　　　　　　　　　　　　　　小李

　　　　　　　　　　　　　　　　　　　　　三點十分

(　　) 1. 小張想請小王一個人吃飯。

(　　) 2. 這個星期六小張要去飯館吃餃子。

(　　) 3. 小張要小王給他打電話。

(　　) 4. 小張現在不在家。

(　　) 5. 小王三點十分給小李打電話。

E. Translate the note above into English.

IV. Writing and Grammar Exercises

Section One

A. Following the model, rewrite the sentences below.

   Example: 我今年夏天沒有看電影。
      ===>我今年夏天一個電影都(也)沒有看。

1. 他今天早上沒有吃東西。

2. 飯館裏人很多，沒有位子了。

3. 我最近忙極了，沒有時間。

4. 這篇課文的生詞又多又難，我不懂。

5. 昨天晚上我忙極了，沒睡覺。

B. Answer the following questions.

1. *A：* 你覺得是中餐好吃還是西餐好吃？

   B： _____ 。

2. *A：* 要是你不能吃味精，你可以跟服務員說什麼？

   B： _____ 。

3. *A：* 今天我請客，你要點些什麼菜？

   B： _____ 。

4. *A：* 要是你餓極了，你可以跟服務員說什麼？

   B： _____ 。

5. *A：* 在美國是吃飯以前喝酒，還是吃飯以後喝酒？

   B： _____ 。

6. *A：* 天氣熱的時候，你喜歡吃什麼？喝什麼？

   B： _____ 。

C. Fill in the blanks, using the English in the parentheses as a clue:

A： 兩杯啤酒三塊八，一瓶可樂一塊錢，_____ (total) 四塊八。

B： 這是十塊錢。

A： _____ (give you change) 六塊二。

B： 謝謝。哦，_____ (you gave the wrong change)。應該找我五塊二，

可是你 _____ (you gave me one dollar too much)。

D. Fill in the blanks with proper resultative complements:

1. 爸爸：小明，功課做得怎麼樣了？

    小明：功課還沒做_____。

2. *A:* 老師說的話你聽_____了嗎？

    B: 老師說話說得太快，我沒_____。

3. *A:* 師傅，還有酸辣湯嗎？

    B: 對不起，已經賣_____了。

4. 這個字不對，你寫_____了。

E. Complete and expand the dialogue:

男客人：_____ ？

服務生：對不起，糖醋魚沒有了，紅燒牛肉可以嗎？

男客人：也可以。

服務生：除了紅燒牛肉以外，_____ ？

女客人：老王，_____ ？

男客人：好，_____ 。

服務生：一盤紅燒牛肉，兩碗酸辣湯，_____ ？

男客人：_____ 。

女客人：我不要米飯。

F. Translate the following sentences into Chinese.

1. Bring us two glasses of beer. (來)

2. Do you want to have dinner at home or go to a restaurant? (想; 還是)

3. *A:* How many classes do you have today?

   B: I don't have a single class today. (一...都/也...)

4. *A:* Do you have any Japanese books?

   B: No, I don't have a single Japanese book. (一...都/也...)

5. Waiter： Do you want anything else?

   Customer： Yes, give me a bottle of cola, please. (來)

6. *A:* How do you like the hot-and-sour soup? (覺得)

B: It's a bit sour and a bit hot. Very tasty. (reduplication of adj.)

7. The beef braised in brown sauce is extremely good. Why don't you buy one?
   (…極了)

8. This book is extremely interesting.

9. *A:* Did I write this character right? (resultative complement)

   B: No, you wrote it wrong. (resultative complement)

10. Sorry! Sweet-and-sour fish is sold out!

11. The home-style tofu is extremely tasty! (. . . 極了)

12. You gave me fifty cents too much for the change.

Section Two

A. Write down the names of your favorite Chinese dishes.

B. Write a letter to your Chinese friend describing the situation when you and your classmate had a meal at a Chinese restaurant. Don't forget to use the following words: 湯、菜、飯。

C. Write a story based on the picture below.

Lesson Thirteen   At the Library

I. Listening Comprehension

Section One (Listen to the tape for the textbook)

A. Dialogue I (Multiple choice)
( ) 1. What does the student wish to borrow?
      a. books   b. tapes   c. records   d. dictionaries

( ) 2. What did the student bring to the library?
      a. a student ID   b. a library card
      c. a credit card   d. a book

( ) 3. When did the student talk to the library staff?
      a. 4:30   b. 5:00   c. 5:30   d. 8:00

( ) 4. What is downstairs in the library?
      a. a reading room   b. a reference room
      c. a language lab   d. a computer room

B. Dialogue II (True/False)
( ) 1. This library is an open-shelf library.
( ) 2. When checking out books, you need to present your library card as well as your student ID.
( ) 3. You can check out a book for eight months at a time at this library.
( ) 4. The overdue penalty is fifty cents per day.
( ) 5. You can only check out dictionaries on weekends.

Section Two (Listen to the tape for the workbook)
A. Narrative (True/False)
( ) 1. In a Chinese college library, the students have to ask the librarian to look for the books they want to borrow.
( ) 2. In a Chinese college library, a student does not need any ID to check out books.
( ) 3. In a Chinese college library, a student cannot renew the books he/she checked out.

B. Dialogue (True/False)
( ) 1. The conversation took place inside the library.
( ) 2. No audiotapes are allowed to leave the library.
( ) 3. The man is a teacher.
( ) 4. The man wishes to check out some audiotapes.
( ) 5. The language lab is right next door to the library.

II. Speaking Exercises

Section One (Answer the questions in Chinese based on the texts)

A. Dialogue I
1. What does the man wish to borrow?
2. Where is the language lab?
3. What did the man forget to bring?
4. Did the man bring any ID with him?
5. How late does the language lab stay open?
6. When did the conversation take place?

B. Dialogue II
1. What does the man wish to borrow?
2. Is the man allowed to go in the stacks to look for books? How do you know?
3. What does the man need to have to borrow books?
4. What will happen to the man if he fails to return books on time?
5. Can he borrow dictionaries?

Section Two

A. You are studying Chinese in China. You go to the library to borrow books, but you don't know how to check out a book. You ask the librarian for help. You would like to know how many books you can check out each time, how long you can keep the books, and what identification you need for checking out books.

B. Ask your friend if you can check out videotapes from the language lab, how long you can keep the tapes each time, what ID you need to check out tapes and if you can renew them.

C. Tell a story based on the picture below.

III. Reading Comprehension

Section One (Answer the questions about the dialogues)

A. Dialogue I

1. 這個學生要借什麼？

2. 學生可以把錄音帶借回家嗎？你怎麼知道？

3. 學生和職員在哪兒說話？

4. 學生忘了什麼？

5. 學生帶了什麼證件？

6. 圖書館開到幾點？

7. 他們說話的時候是幾點鐘？

8. 學生今天借到了他要的東西嗎？你怎麼知道？

B. Dialogue II

1. 這個學生要借什麼？

2. 學生可以自己進去找他要的東西嗎？

3. 學生借書的時候得用什麼證件？

4. 書可以借多久？

5. 要是過期兩天得罰多少錢？

6. 書可以續借嗎？

7. 學生可以把字典借回家嗎？

Section Two

A. Read the following passage and answer the questions. (True/False)

在美國的大學圖書館借書，老師、研究生和大學生一次可以借的時間不一樣。老師可以借一年，研究生可以借半年，大學生只能借一個月。借的書，只要沒有人要借，都可以續借，很方便。

( ) 1. 老師借書一次可以借十二個月。

( ) 2. 老師、研究生和大學生借了書都可以續借。

( ) 3. 大學生一次只可以借一本書。

( ) 4. 如果一位大學生借一本書要借十個星期，他得續借兩次。

( ) 5. 研究生借書可以比大學生多借四個月。

B. Read the following passage and answer the questions. (True/False)

老師說要想中文進步得快，最好的辦法就是天天聽錄音。他告訴我們中文錄音帶都在語言實驗室，但是不能借回家去，只能在那兒聽。語言實驗室除了星期六以外每天都開。而且早上七點半就開門，晚上九點半才關門。老師還告訴我們去借錄音帶的時候不要忘了帶借書證。

( ) 1. 老師覺得聽錄音帶是學中文的好辦法。

( ) 2. 學生可以把錄音帶借回家聽。

( ) 3. 語言實驗室一星期開五天。

( ) 4. 早上八點一刻，語言實驗室已經開了。

( ) 5. 借錄音帶的時候要看學生證。

IV. Writing and Grammar Exercises

Section One

A. Following the model, rewrite each of the sentences below into one that contains the 把 structure.

       Example: 我帶來了你的一本書。

            ===>我把你的那本書帶來了。

1. 我還給了圖書館一本書。

2. 他開走了王朋的汽車。

3. 他借回來了錄音帶。

4. 他寫錯了字。

5. 我看完了這本書。

6. 你沒有給我你的借書證。

7. 他給了女朋友一張電影票。

8. 我買回來一個電腦。

B. Complete the following sentences with 如果/ 要是…最好

1. 如果你借的書過期了，＿＿＿＿＿＿＿＿＿＿＿＿＿＿＿＿＿＿。

2. 如果是明天下午有空，＿＿＿＿＿＿＿＿＿＿＿＿＿＿＿＿＿。

3. 如果想學好中文，＿＿＿＿＿＿＿＿＿＿＿＿＿＿＿＿＿＿＿。

4. ＿＿＿＿＿＿＿＿＿＿＿＿＿＿＿＿＿＿＿，我可以借給你。

5. ＿＿＿＿＿＿＿＿＿＿＿＿＿＿＿＿＿，別忘了帶證件。

C. Fill in the blanks using the clue in the parentheses.

1. 請你在餐廳 ＿＿＿＿＿＿＿＿＿＿＿＿＿＿＿＿＿＿＿ (wait for a while).

2. 請問，這本書可以 ＿＿＿＿＿＿＿＿＿＿＿＿ (how long can I borrow)?

3. 請你把錄音帶＿＿＿＿＿＿＿＿＿＿＿＿＿＿＿(return to the library).

4. 你把學生證 ＿＿＿＿＿＿＿＿＿＿＿＿＿＿＿＿＿＿＿＿＿
   (Where did you put your student ID) ?

D. Answer the following questions using 把.
1. *A:* 我的中文書在哪兒？

   B: ＿＿＿＿＿＿＿＿＿＿＿＿＿＿＿＿＿＿＿。（放在）

2.（正在吃飯）

    A: 媽媽，我可以出去玩嗎？

    B: _____。（吃完）

3. *A:* 已經十二點了，快睡覺吧！

    B: _____。（預習好）

4. *A:* 你借的錄音帶在哪兒？我想聽一下。

    B: 那盤錄音帶明天就過期了，_____。（還給）

E.　Put the following sentences into the correct order.

1. 在學生餐廳　　今天早上　　我　　一杯　喝了　咖啡。

2. 跟小李　　他　　打球　昨天下午　　一個鐘頭　　打了。

3. 我弟弟　　寫了　用中文　　昨天晚上　　寫信　三十分鐘。

4. 王老師　　二十分鐘　　第一節課　　教了　教發音。

F. Translate the following sentences into Chinese.

1. He ate his breakfast for two hours, and did not finish it until 10 o'clock.
   (duration; V + 到)

2. They danced for five hours last night. (duration)

3. *A:* You wrote this character wrong. How long have you studied Chinese?

   B: Twenty years. But only for one week each year. (duration)

4. Would you wait here for a little while? (能不能 ，V + 一下)

5. Please put your library card on the table.

6. I waited for my girlfriend's phone call until eleven o'clock last night.

7. I returned the dictionary to her this morning. (把)

8. The language laboratory is upstairs.

9. Do you have any other ID in addition to a student ID? (除了...以外)

10. How late does the library stay open? (V + 到)

Section Two

A. Write a letter to a library in Chinese to find out how to borrow books, how many
    books you can check out at a time and for how long, and what the fine is if the books
    are overdue.

B. Write a note to your Chinese friend, explaining to him/her how to borrow tapes at
    your language lab.

Lesson Fourteen   Asking Directions

I. Listening Comprehension

Section One (Listen to the tape for the textbook)

A. Dialogue I (Multiple choice)

(   ) 1. Where is the man going?
        a. library   b. student activities center   c. computer center   d. bookstore

(   ) 2. Where is the woman going?
        a. library   b. student activities center   c. computer center   d. bookstore

(   ) 3. Which of the following places is the closest to the bookstore?
        a. athletic field b. computer center c. student activities center   d. library

(   ) 4. Which of the following places is the farthest away from the two speakers?
        a. athletic field b. computer center c. student activities center   d. library

B. Dialogue II (True/False)
(   ) 1. The man has never been to Chinatown.
(   ) 2. The woman is asking the man to give her a ride.
(   ) 3. The woman has a map.
(   ) 4. According to the dialogue, they finally get to Chinatown.

Section Two (Listen to the tape for the workbook)

A. Dialogue I   (True/False)
(   ) 1. The library is to the north of the dormitory.
(   ) 2. The woman now knows where she took a wrong turn a moment ago.
(   ) 3. To get to the library, the woman needs to make a right turn first, then a left turn.
(   ) 4. There is no traffic light between the dormitory and the library.

B. Narrative (Listen to the narrative and identify the buildings in the picture on p.24.)

(   ) 1. Dormitory
(   ) 2. Library
(   ) 3. Student activities center
(   ) 4. Computer center
(   ) 5. Classroom

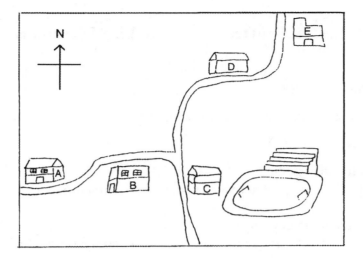

II. Speaking Exercises

Section One (Answer the questions in Chinese based on the texts.)

A. Dialogue I
1. Where is Mr. Jin going?
2. Has Mr. Jin been to the computer center before? Please explain.
3. Which one is farther, the computer center or the sports field?
4. Where is the computer center?
5. Where is Miss Tian going?
6. Why did Mr. Jin say that had he known it earlier, he would not have asked for the directions?

B. Dialogue II
1. Does Old Wang know how to get to Chinatown? Please explain.
2. Who has a map, Old Wang or Old Li?
3. Where were the speakers at the beginning of the conversation, north of Chinatown or south of Chinatown?
4. How many intersections do they need to pass before they reach Chinatown?
5. What did they do when they found out that the street which they were supposed to turn onto was a one-way street?
6. Did they eventually reach Chinatown? Please explain.

Section Two

A. You are a new student at a Chinese school. Ask your fellow student how to get to the classroom from the dormitory. And find out the locations of the library and the student union in relation to the classroom.

B. Your Chinese roommate has just arrived on campus. Please explain to her/him how to get to the library, the student activities center, and the athletic field from the dormitory.

III. Reading Comprehension

Section One (Answer the questions about the dialogues)

A. Dialogue I

1. 老金想去哪裏？

2. 他知道怎麼走嗎？

3. 電腦中心旁邊有什麼？

4. 書店在哪兒？

5. 爲什麼金先生，田小姐要一起走？

B. Dialogue II

1. 老王要去哪裏？

2. 爲什麼他要老李告訴他怎麼走？

3. 爲什麼第四個路口只能往左拐？

4. 最後老王和老李到了什麼地方？

Section Two

A. Read the following passage and answer the questions.

> 小田家離學校很遠。每天早上，他得走十五分鐘到火車站，再坐一小時火車到台南。學校就在火車站旁邊，下火車後，不用走太久。因為走路和坐火車上學得花很多時間，所以他想下學期在學校住。

1. 小田住在台南嗎？你怎麼知道？

2. 小田每天上學要花多少時間？

3. 小田下火車後要走很久嗎？爲什麼？

4. 爲什麼小田想在學校住？

B. Read the following passage and answer the questions.

> 老李在紐約住了八年了，週末常常到中國城去買東西、吃中國飯。因爲每次去中國城都是坐朋友的車，所以有一次他自己開車到中國城去就迷路了。最後只好去問人，別人告訴他怎麼走以後，他就找到了。

1. 老李知道怎麼去中國城嗎？你怎麼知道？

2. 老李常去中國城做什麼？

3. 最後老李怎麼找到了中國城？

C. Answer the following true-or-false questions according to the map.

(　) 1. 公園在老金家的東邊。

(　) 2. 醫院在電影院的南邊。

(　) 3. 圖書館在醫院的西邊。

(　) 4. 公園的北邊有車站。

(　) 5. 飯店離老金家很近。

(　) 6. 學校和電影院的中間是書店。

D. Fill in the letters according to the given information.

宿舍在車站的南邊。宿舍的西邊是圖書館。電影院在圖書館的西北邊。學生活動中心在電影院和公園的中間。醫院在宿舍的南邊。

a: 圖書館   b: 宿舍   c: 電影院   d: 學生活動中心   e: 醫院

IV. Writing and Grammar Exercises

Section One

A. Make questions using the given words, and also answer the questions.

> Example: 學校/ 中國城
>
> ===>學校離中國城遠不遠？
>
> ===> 學校離中國城不遠 。

1. 宿舍/ 學生活動中心。

===>

===>

2. 圖書館/ 運動場。

===>

===>

3. 書店/ 電腦中心。

===>

===>

4. 你的家 / 電影院。

===>

===>

5. 美國 / 中國。

===>

===>

6. 上海 / 台北。

===>

===>

B. Follow the model and make comparative sentences using the given words.

　　　Example: 英文 / 日文 = = = > 英文沒有日文那麼難。 / 英文比日文容易。

1. 說中文 / 寫漢字

2. 住在宿舍 / 住在家裏

3. 學校的飯 / 飯館的飯

4. 東京 / 台北

5. 走路 / 開車

6. 男孩子 / 女孩子

C. Answer the following questions using the English phrase in the parentheses as a clue.

1. *A:* 學校的書店在哪裏？

　　B: _____ (inside the student union) 。

2. *A:* 我的書哪兒去了？

　　B: _____ (under the table) 。

3. *A:* 請問運動場離這兒遠不遠？

   B: 不遠，_____
       (just between the computer center and the library) 。

4. *A:* 你的宿舍在哪兒?

   B: _____ (beside the school's bookstore)。

5. *A:* 我們到哪兒去打球？

   B: _____
       (the sports field outside the classroom) 。

D. Answer the following questions using the given words and sentence pattern.
    Sentence pattern: 一直往_____，到_____，往_____就到了。

1. 請問到學校的書店怎麼走？（南，第二個路口，西）

2. 到電影院怎麼走？（前，第三個紅綠燈，右）

3. 請問到運動場怎麼走？（東，圖書館，北）

4. 到中國城怎麼走？（前，有中國字的地方，左。）

E. Answer the following questions using 過.

     Example: 台北夏天熱不熱？

          ===> 我不知道，因爲我沒去過台北。

1. 日文語法難不難？

2. 上海人多不多？

3. 那個中國電影好看嗎？

4. 跳舞有意思嗎？

5. 紅葉好看嗎？

F . Fill in the blanks with resultative complements.

1. 老師說的語法你聽＿＿＿＿＿＿＿＿＿了嗎？

2. 老師，這個漢字我沒寫＿＿＿＿＿＿＿＿＿，您再看看。

3. 今天看電影的人很多，我沒買＿＿＿＿＿＿＿電影票。

4. 妹妹說她寫＿＿＿＿＿＿＿信就跟我去打球。

5. 你去中國的機票買＿＿＿＿＿＿＿了嗎？

G. Use the given words to make sentences with the expression "一 ... 就 ..."
　　　Example: 我回家以後就開始預習功課。
　　　===> 我一回家就預習功課。

1. 今天我起床以後就聽錄音。

2. 這一課很容易，我看了一下就懂了。

3. 活動中心不遠，往前走到路口，再往左拐就到了。

4. 這本書很多人想借，請你看完就還給我。

5. 我給媽媽買了一件衣服，買好了就給她了。

H. Translate the following into Chinese.

1. The language laboratory is very far from here. （離）

2. Have you ever seen that videotape? （過）

3. Walk straight north and you will get to the computer center. （一直，就）

4. *A:* Is the library far away from the athletic field? （離）

    B: The library is not that far. （那麼）

5. Go straight north from your dorm, make a left turn at the first intersection, and you will be there. （一直，往 . . . 拐，就）

6. Her Japanese is very good. She has read many Japanese books. （過）

7. I'll go shopping if it's a nice day tomorrow. (就)

8. If next week is colder than this week, I'll study in the library. （比，就）

9. As soon as I find the dictionary, I'll give you a call. （一... 就）

10. I understood him the moment he said it. （一... 就）

11. He went to the sports field to play ball.

12. Were you able to buy that book successfully?

Section Two

A. Draw a map of your school campus labeling it in Chinese, and describe the best way to get to the library, the student activities center, and the computer center from your dormitory.

B. Write a paragraph telling your Chinese friend how to get to your home / dormitory from the airport / bus stop / train station.

Lesson Fifteen   Birthday Party

I. Listening Comprehension

Section One (Listen to the tape for the textbook)

A. Dialogue I (Multiple choice)

(   ) 1. What was Wang Peng doing when Li You called him?
      a. dancing   b. singing   c. eating   d. reading

(   ) 2. When is Little Lin's birthday?
      a. yesterday   b. today   c. tomorrow   d. day after tomorrow

(   ) 3. What time will the party start?
      a. 7:00   b. 8:00   c. 9:00   d. 10:00

(   ) 4. What will Wang Peng bring to the party?
      a. snacks   b. soda   c. fruit   d. juice

(   ) 5. How will Wang Peng get to the party?
      a. by driving his own car   b. by bus
      c. by riding in Li You's car   d. by walking

B. Dialogue II (Multiple choice)

(   ) 1. Whose birthday was it?
      a. Wang Peng's   b. Li You's
      c. Little Lin's   d. Helen's

(   ) 2. Whom did Wang Peng meet at the party?
      a. Little Lin's cousin   b. Li You's cousin
      c. Little Lin's sister   d. Li You's sister

(   ) 3. What is Tom's sign in the Chinese Zodiac?
      a. dog   b. ox   c. horse   d. tiger

(   ) 4. Why will Tom be handsome in the future?
      a. His father is handsome   b. His mother is pretty
      c. Tom has a beautiful nose d. Tom has beautiful eyes

(   ) 5. What shall Tom study in the future?
      a. Chinese b. English c. piano   d. violin

Section Two (Listen to the tape for the workbook) (Multiple choice)

A. Dialogue I (Multiple choice)

(   ) 1. This dialogue is most likely to have occurred_____.
      a. at a birthday party
      b. on the phone
      c. in a classroom

(   ) 2. Which of the following statements is true?
        a. Li You does not know what day tomorrow is.
        b. Li You does not know what date tomorrow is.
        c. Li You is not asking what day or what date tomorrow is.

(   ) 3. How did Li You discover that it is Wang Peng's birthday?
        a. He told her earlier in her car.
        b. She learned that from his student ID.
        c. She learned that from some of his friends.

(   ) 4. Wang Peng says that he did not know that the next day was his birthday because
        he _____.
        a. had been too busy and forgot about it.
        b. did not want to celebrate his birthday.
        c. was confused about the day's date.

(   ) 5. What are they going to do at tomorrow's party?
        a. have dinner and then dance.
        b. have a reception followed by a dinner.
        c. have dinner and then watch a movie.

B. Dialogue (Multiple choice)

(   ) 1. Why were they talking about Wang Peng's parents?
        Because _____ .
        a. they showed up at the party.
        b. they sent their recent photo to Wang Peng.
        c. they appear in a photo that was taken many years ago.

(   ) 2. According to the dialogue, who does Wang Peng take after?
        a. His mother.
        b. His father.
        c. Both his parents.

II. Speaking Exercises

Section One (Answer the questions in Chinese based on the texts

A. Dialogue I

1. Why did Li You talk to Wang Peng?
2. What will happen at Little Lin's home tonight? Please provide as many details as possible.

3. Who will go to Little Lin's home tonight?
4. What will Wang Peng bring to Little Lin's house?
5. Why didn't Wang Peng want Li You to give him a ride?

B. Dialogue II

1. Who asked about Wang Peng before he arrived? Why?
2. What did Wang Peng say to Little Lin when he entered Little Lin's house? How did Little Lin reply?
3. Did Wang Peng arrive early or late? How do you know?
4. Did Wang Peng meet anyone at Little Lin's house?
5. What did Li You tell Helen about Wang Peng?
6. Does Helen speak Chinese? Please explain.
7. Who is Tom? What can you tell us about him? Can you describe Tom's appearance?
8. Why did Li You say that Tom should study piano? Please explain.

Section Two

A. Describe one of your friends or relatives, including his or her age, personality, appearance, family background, hobbies, etc.

B. Call your friend or relative, invite him/her to a party, and tell him/her what the arrangements are. Tell him/her how to get to your house. Each of your classmates may play a role.

C. Tell a story based on the picture below.

III. Reading Comprehension

Section One (Answer the questions about the dialogues)

A. Dialogue I

1. 李友打電話給王朋的時候，他正在做什麼？

2. 李友今天晚上七點鐘有什麼事？

3. 小林是男的還是女的？

4. 開舞會以前他們先做什麼？

5. 為什麼王朋要帶果汁？

6. 誰要走路去小林家？為什麼？

B.   Dialogue II

1. 王朋為什麼去小林家？

2. 王朋送給小林什麼？

3. 海倫是誰？湯姆是誰？湯姆多大？

4. 海倫是王朋的同學，對不對？你怎麼知道？

5. 海倫是在哪兒學的中文？

6. 為什麼小林說湯姆將來一定很帥？

7. 湯姆長得像誰？

8. 湯姆將來會很高嗎？

9. 湯姆將來應該學什麼？為什麼？

10. 湯姆是屬什麼的？

Section Two

A. Read the following passage and answer the questions. (True/False)

昨天是小金二十歲生日，晚上我們在他的宿舍給他過生日。大家給他買了一張卡片。小金的女朋友買了果汁，汽水（兒），還有很多好吃的東西。大家一邊吃東西一邊玩，一直玩到十二點多才回家，所以我的功課沒做完，今天的考試也考得糟糕極了。

(   ) 1. 小金今年二十歲。

(   ) 2. 小金跟他的爸爸媽媽一起住在家裏。

(   ) 3. 生日卡，果汁和汽水（兒）都是大家一起買的。

(   ) 4. 小金是男的。

(   ) 5. 今天的考試小金考得很不好。

B. Read the following passage and answer the questions. (True/False)

小高很喜歡她日文班的一個很帥的男同學。那個男同學跟小高一樣，是美國人。他的眼睛是藍色的，鼻子高高的，笑的時候很好看。他又會唱歌又會彈鋼琴。下個星期六學校有個舞會，小高很想請他一起去跳舞，可是不好意思問他。

(   ) 1. 小高喜歡的男學生也學日文。

(   ) 2. 小高是美國人。

(   ) 3. 那個男同學的眼睛是黑色的。

(   ) 4. 下個星期六小高家裏有個舞會。

(   ) 5. 那個男同學請小高跟他去跳舞。

IV. Writing and Grammar Exercises

Section One

A. Following the English directions, use the structures "是 . . . 的" or "了" to ask and answer questions based on the passage below.

> 15 B王朋和李友昨天晚上從學校開車到電影院去看電影。看完電影以後，他們走路到電影院附近的一個中國飯館去吃晚飯。吃飯的時候他們喝了一點兒酒。

1. Find out if Wang Peng went to the movies last night.

   Q: _____ 。

   A: _____ 。

2. Find out who went together with Wang Peng.

   Q: _____ 。

   A: _____ 。

3. Find out how they went to the movie theater.

   Q: _____ 。

   A: _____ 。

4. Find out from where they went to the movie theater.

   Q: _____ 。

A: _____ 。

5. Find out if Wang Peng and Li You ate dinner last night.

   Q: _____ 。

   A: _____ 。

6. Find out where Wang Peng and Li You ate dinner last night.

   Q: _____ 。

   A: _____ 。

7. Find out how Wang Peng and Li You went to the restaurant.

   Q: _____ 。

   A: _____ 。

8. Find out if Wang Peng and Li You drank last night.

   Q: _____ 。

   A: _____ 。

9. Find out where Wang Peng and Li You drank wine last night.

   Q: _____ 。

   A: _____ 。

B. Fill in the appropriate blanks with 了、過 or 是...的. Put X in the unfilled blanks.

1. *A:* 小張_____來_____嗎？

   B: 來了。

   A: 小張_____什麼時候來_____？

   B: 昨天晚上來_____。

   A: 小張_____以前來_____嗎？

   B: 沒有。

2. *A:* 這是你的書吧？

   B: 對，是我的。

   A: 你_____什麼時候買_____？

   B: 去年買_____。

   A: 在哪兒買_____？

   B: 在中國買_____，你看_____這本書嗎？

   A: 沒看_____，我以前不知道有這本書。

C. Complete the following sentences using 一定.

1. 你的弟弟從小喜歡運動，_____。(athlete)

2. 這個學生又會中文，又會英文，又會法文，_____。(smart)

3. 他平常不喜歡練習說中文，也不喜歡練習寫漢字，_____。
   (in a terrible mess)

4. 他父親天天去中國飯館吃飯，_____。(like)

D. Use the pivotal construction "Noun + Verb + Noun + Verb" to ask and answer
    questions about the underlined part in each of the following sentences. You can use
    the following verbs: 讓，請，叫，要

> Example: 媽媽   妹妹   <u>學鋼琴/ 看電視</u>
>
> ===>   *A:* 媽媽讓妹妹做什麼？
>
> *B:* 媽媽讓妹妹學鋼琴。
>
> ===>   *C:* 媽媽不讓妹妹做什麼？
>
> *D:* 媽媽不讓妹妹看電視。

1. 老師   學生   在語言實驗室<u>看錄像</u>/ <u>聊天兒</u>

   A:

   B:

   C:

   D:

2. 圖書管理員   我   把<u>證件</u>給他/ 把<u>字典</u>帶回家。

   A:

   B:

   C:

   D:

3. 父母   我   用<u>中文</u>給他們寫信/ 用<u>英文</u>給他們寫信

   A:

   B:

C:

D:

4. 醫生　　　　　我哥哥　　　多吃水果/喝酒

　A:

　B:

　C:

　D:

E. Answer the following questions, using the "正在 … 呢" structure.

1. *A:* 今天早上六點，你在做什麼？我給你打電話，可是沒人接。(take a bath)

　B:

2. *A:* 我昨天下午三點來你家，你不在。你上哪兒去了？(take an exam)

　B:

3. *A:* 明天早上九點鐘你有事嗎？你開車帶我去買東西可以嗎？(attend a class)

　B:

4. (打電話)
　A: 你正在做什麼呢？(watch T.V.)

　B:

F. Following the model, combine each pair of sentences into one.

　　Example: 我媽媽做了一個菜。 那個菜很好吃。

　　　　===> 我媽媽做了一個很好吃的菜。

1. 王朋給李友寫了一封信。 那封信很客氣。

2. 我姐姐昨天買了一件新衣服。 那件衣服很好看。

3. 黃先生上個星期認識了一個朋友。 那個朋友在日本工作。

4. 小張借了一本書。 那本書又難懂又沒有意思。

5. 我有一個表姐。 她會彈鋼琴。

G. Complete the following sentences using 還.

1. A: 我們出去打球好嗎？

　　B: 等一下，＿＿＿＿＿＿＿＿＿＿＿＿＿＿＿＿＿＿＿＿＿＿。（吃飯）

2. (打電話)

　　A: 喂，王朋在家嗎？

　　B: 他在家，可是＿＿＿＿＿＿＿＿＿＿＿＿＿＿＿＿＿＿。（起床）

3. A: 你怎麼不睡覺？

　　B: 我不能睡，＿＿＿＿＿＿＿＿＿＿＿＿＿＿＿＿＿＿＿。（功課）

4. A：李友回來了嗎？

　　B：沒有，＿＿＿＿＿＿＿＿＿＿＿＿＿＿＿＿＿＿＿＿＿。（在小林家跳舞）

H.　Translate the following into Chinese.

1.　I will eat first and then go to play ball. (先 . . . 再. . .)

2.　The girl who danced with you last night was my cousin.

3.　I will go to China for sure in the future. (將來，一定)

4.　It's already 10:30.　How come Little Lin still hasn't come?

5.　We had our dancing party at my boyfriend's home. (是 . . . 的)

6.　Who gave you this birthday present? (是 . . . 的)

7.　She either plays the piano or goes to dance on weekends; she doesn't like to watch
　　TV. (或者)

8.　What is the salesperson saying? (在 . . . 呢)

9. My younger brother asked me to call him tomorrow. (pivotal sentence)

10. Her eyes are big and her nose is high, and she looks very much like her mother. (reduplication of adj., 像)

11. Where did you meet him? (認識，是...的)

12. How old is your younger sister? What is her sign in the Chinese zodiac? (屬)

Section Two

A. Write a letter inviting your friend to attend your birthday party. Tell him/her what activities you will have at the party. Don't forget to tell him/her the date, time and place.

B. Write a paragraph describing the appearance of a family member. Make sure that you describe his/her eyes, nose, height, legs, fingers, etc.

Lesson Sixteen　　　Seeing a Doctor

I. Listening Comprehension

Section One (Listen to the tape for the textbook) (Multiple choice)

A. Dialogue I (Multiple choice)

(　　) 1.　Why did the man go to see the doctor?
        a.　He had a cold.
        b.　He had a stomachache.
        c.　He injured his hand.
        e.　He injured his leg.

(　　) 2.　What caused the man's problem?
        a.　Insufficient sleep.
        b.　A basketball game.
        c.　A soccer match.
        d.　Leftover food.

(　　) 3.　What is the treatment for the man's problem?
        a.　To take a shot and some medicine.
        b.　To stay home and rest.
        c.　To have physical therapy and take medicine.
        d.　To take medicine only.

(　　) 4.　How many pills does the man need to take daily?
        a.　2
        b.　3
        c.　5
        d.　6

(　　) 5.　What is the doctor's suggestion to the man?
        a.　stop playing basketball for three months.
        b.　no more soccer games.
        c.　fast for one day.
        d.　drink plenty of liquids.

B.　Dialogue II
(　　) 1.　The woman cried because she was homesick.
(　　) 2.　The man is allergic to flowers.
(　　) 3.　The woman will go to the pharmacy tomorrow to buy four kinds of medicine.
(　　) 4.　The man advised the woman to go to see a doctor right away.
(　　) 5.　The woman has no health insurance.
(　　) 6.　The woman is a doctor.

Section Two (Listen to the tape for the workbook)

A. Dialogue I (True/False)

(   ) 1. Li You has not seen Wang Peng for a few days.
(   ) 2. Wang Peng has been suffering from a cold these days.
(   ) 3. Wang Peng does not need to see the doctor because he has some Chinese
            medicine that he has brought from China.
(   ) 4. Wang Peng is feeling much better today.

B. Dialogue II (Multiple choice)

(   ) 1. According to the doctor, which of the following statements is true?
            a. The patient is seriously ill.
            b. The patient is not ill at all.
            c. The patient is ill, but the problem is not serious.

(   ) 2. What does the doctor think of the patient's dinner yesterday?
            a. He thinks the patient should have eaten three bowls of dumplings.
            b. He thinks the patient should have eaten less rice but more beef.
            c. He thinks the patient should not have eaten so much.

(   ) 3. How many tablets is the patient supposed to take daily?
            a. 3   b. 6   c. 9

C. Narrative (True/False)

(   ) 1. In China, people go to see a doctor only when they are seriously ill.
(   ) 2. In China, a doctor's consultation is inexpensive, but the prices for medicine are
            extremely high.
(   ) 3. Medical insurance in the U.S. is very expensive because people go to see a doctor
            even for small ailments.

II. Speaking Exercises

Section One (Answer the questions in Chinese based on the texts)

A. Dialogue I

1. Why did the patient go to see the doctor?
2. What happened to the patient yesterday?
3. What did the doctor do after listening to the patient?
4. How is the doctor going to treat the patient?
5. How should the patient take the medicine?
6. What is the doctor's suggestion to the patient at the end of the consultation? Is the
    patient willing to do what the doctor recommended? Please explain.

B. Dialogue II

1. Why does Little Xie have red eyes?

2. How did Little Xie try to treat her allergy?
3. Why did the man ask Little Xie to see a doctor right away?
4. Is Little Xie willing to see a doctor? Please explain.

Section Two

A. You came home last night around nine o'clock, and were very hungry. You saw some leftover food on the table and you ate it. Around midnight you started to have a stomachache and you had to go to the bathroom many times throughout the night. Explain to your doctor what happened, and ask him/her if there is any medicine that you can take to treat your problem. Don't forget to ask the doctor how to take the medicine.

B. Call your teacher to tell him/her that you are not able to go to school because you caught a cold and are running a fever and have a bad cough.

C. Tell a story based on the picture below.

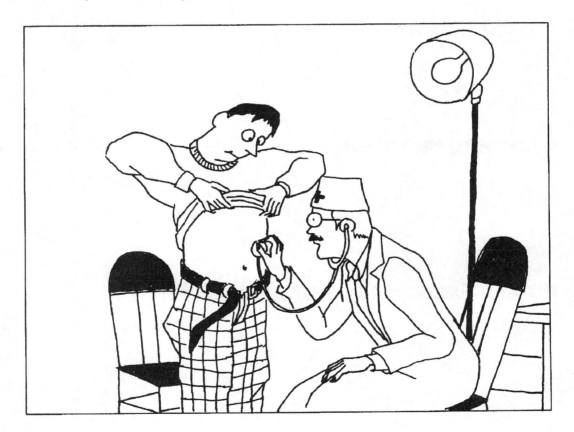

III. Reading Comprehension

Section One (Answer the questions about the dialogues)

A. Dialogue I

1. 病人什麼地方不舒服？

2. 病人昨天吃什麼東西了？

3. 醫生說病人是什麼病？

4. 病人得打針和吃藥嗎？藥怎麼吃？

5. 醫生說最好的辦法是什麼？病人覺得那個辦法好嗎？為什麼？

B. Dialogue II

1. 小謝爲什麼眼睛紅紅的？

2. 小謝的身體哪兒不舒服？怎麼不舒服？

3. 小謝是在哪裏買的藥？

4. 小謝爲什麼買了四、五種藥？

5. 小謝上次生病去看醫生了沒有？

6. 小謝爲什麼不去看醫生？

Section Two

A. Read the following passage and answer the questions.(True/False)

> 因為今天要考試，小馬昨天晚上看書看到今天早上四點才睡覺，六點就起床了。一起床他就覺得頭有一點兒疼。吃早飯以後，小馬頭越來越疼，不能去上課。小馬的媽媽帶他去看醫生。醫生說小馬沒什麼問題，只是睡覺不夠，好好睡兩天就會好了。醫生沒有給他打針，也沒給他藥吃。

(   ) 1. 因為昨天小馬考試考得不好，所以今天他頭疼。

(   ) 2. 媽媽帶小馬去看醫生。

(   ) 3. 小馬沒有病，只是睡覺不夠。

(   ) 4. 醫生給了小馬一些藥，但是沒給他打針。

B. Read the following passage and answer the questions. (True/False)

> 小錢住在學校外邊，她喜歡自己做飯。但是這個星期她的功課很多，沒有時間做飯，就每天到學校的餐廳吃飯。今天中午她吃了一盤紅燒牛肉，還喝了一碗酸辣湯。雖然很便宜，可是不太好吃。回家以後她的肚子很不舒服，上了好幾次廁所。下午她的肚子疼極了，就去看醫生。醫生說她吃壞肚子了。小錢說她以後不去餐廳吃飯了，還是自己做飯好。

(   ) 1. 小錢住在學校的宿舍裏。

(   ) 2. 小錢去餐廳吃飯是因為她很不喜歡自己做飯。

(   ) 3. 餐廳的飯又貴又不好吃。

(   ) 4. 小錢肚子不舒服因為中午吃的飯有問題。

(   ) 5. 醫生叫小錢以後不要到餐廳去吃飯。

IV. Writing and Grammar Exercises

Section One

A. Fill in the blanks, using the English phrase in the parentheses as a clue.

1. 他上個星期＿＿＿＿＿＿＿＿＿＿＿＿＿＿＿＿＿＿。(went to Chinatown twice)

2. 這種藥 ＿＿＿＿＿＿＿＿＿＿＿＿＿＿＿＿？ (to take how many times per day)

3. 我弟弟肚子不舒服，一個鐘頭就 ＿＿＿＿＿＿＿＿＿＿＿＿＿＿＿＿＿＿。
   (went to the rest room several times)

4. 我和我的朋友想明年 ＿＿＿＿＿＿＿＿＿＿＿＿＿＿＿。(go to Japan once)

5. 姐姐生病了，我想 ＿＿＿＿＿＿＿＿＿＿＿。 (go to see her once every day)

6. 老李＿＿＿＿＿＿＿＿＿＿＿＿＿＿。(call his girlfriend three times a day)

B. Translate the following expressions into Chinese.

1. please sit down:

2. please buy some fruit back:

3. please come in:

4. go upstairs:

5. take out a book:

6. run out of the dorm:

7. walk into the classroom:

8. go into the rest room:

9. come in the computer room:

10. walk downstairs:

C. Answer the following questions.

1. *A:* 你對什麼藥過敏？

   B: _____ 。

2. *A:* 誰對你最好？ 爲什麼？

   B: _____ 。

3. *A:* 哪些練習對你學中文有用？

   B: _____ 。

4. *A:* 喝酒對你身體好嗎？ 爲什麼？

   B: _____ 。

5. *A:* 穿什麼顏色的衣服對你最合適？

   B: _____ 。

D. Complete the following sentences using "要不然" .

1. 你應該每天都聽錄音， _____ 。

2. 生了病應該趕快去看醫生， _____ 。

3. 我明天有一個考試，我要復習一下， _____ 。

4. 你借的書要是到期了，就應該續借， _____ 。

5. 你要天天運動， _____ 。

E. Complete the following sentences with the expression "越來越".

     Example: 現在是十一月了，<u>天氣越來越冷了</u>。（天氣）

1. 第十課以後課文很難，因為_____。
   (more new words)

2. 我不想吃餐廳的飯了，因為_____。
   (the food is getting worse)

3. 我每天都打球，所以_____。
   (become healthier)

4. 我最近不太忙，因為_____。
   (less homework)

5. 他比以前用功，所以_____。
   (do better on tests)

F. Complete the following sentences using the expression 再說.

1. 我不喜歡吃剩菜，因為容易吃壞肚子，_____。
   (does not taste good)

2. 我想明年到中國去，因為老師說中國有很多好玩的地方，_____

   _____。 (can practice Chinese)

3. 我的哥哥喜歡吃中國飯，因為中國飯不太貴，_____。
   (delicious)

4. *A:* 這雙鞋你喜歡不喜歡？

   B: 不喜歡，太貴，＿＿＿＿＿＿＿＿＿＿＿＿＿＿＿＿＿＿＿＿＿ 。(color)

5. *A:* 吃完晚飯以後，你要做什麼？

   B: 我們打球去吧，幾天沒運動了，＿＿＿＿＿＿＿＿＿＿＿＿＿＿＿ 。
      (weather, comfortable)

G. Complete the following short dialogues.

1. *A:* 你是中國人，對不對？

   B:

2. *A:*

   B: 對，我喜歡一邊吃飯一邊看報。

3. *A:* 你很喜歡穿白運動褲，對不對？

   B:

4. *A:*

   B: 不對，台灣的夏天又悶又熱。

H. Translate the following into Chinese.

1. You should go to see a doctor right away; otherwise, your cold will become more and more serious. (越來越..., 要不然)

2. I am not going to see the movie because I don't like movies. Besides, I'm too busy. (再說...也)

3. We need to rush to the pharmacy; otherwise, it will be closed. (要不然)

4. My headache is getting worse. (越來越)

5. I am allergic to this kind of medicine. (對)

6. I have seen that movie five times. (次)

7. The doctor examined the patient for a while. (一下)

8. They stood up and walked out of the classroom. (起來, 走出)

9. Mr. Ma is your teacher, isn't he? (對不對)

10. The students are extremely happy today. (死)

Section Two

A. You are sick, and can't go to school. Write a note to your teacher in Chinese. Tell him/her of your problems and how you got these problems.

B. Write about your health history. Please include the following information:
    --When was the last time you visited a doctor, and why?
    --Are you allergic to any medicine?
    --What kind of treatment do you prefer, getting a shot or taking medicine?
    --Do you have any health insurance?

Lesson Seventeen   Dating

I. Listening Comprehension

Section One (Listen to the tape for the textbook) (Multiple choice)

A. Dialogue I (True/False)

(   ) 1. Wang Peng and Li You are in the same Chinese Class.
(   ) 2. Wang Peng likes Li You, but Li You does not like Wang Peng.
(   ) 3. Wang Peng is inviting Li You to see a Chinese movie.
(   ) 4. After the movie, they will go get something to eat.
(   ) 5. They decided not to go to the movie because the tickets are hard to get.
(   ) 6. They will go to the movie with two other friends.

B. Dialogue II (True/False)

(   ) 1. The woman has never seen the man before.
(   ) 2. The man can dance but not the woman.
(   ) 3. The woman does not remember the man at all.
(   ) 4. The man is inviting the woman to a dance.
(   ) 5. The woman is busy this weekend, but she will go out with the man next weekend.
(   ) 6. The woman does chores at home.

Section Two (Listen to the tape for the workbook)

A. Dialogue I (True/False)

(   ) 1. The woman declined the invitation because she was busy.
(   ) 2. The woman is a student, while the man seems to be a librarian.
(   ) 3. The dialogue occurred at 5:30 p.m.
(   ) 4. The man will call the woman in order to help her return her books to the library.

B. Dialogue II (Multiple choice)

(   ) 1. The man was trying to invite Li You _____.
    a. to dinner
    b. to a dancing party
    c. to see a movie

(   ) 2. Li You says she cannot accept the invitation because she has a prior engagement
    for _____ this evening.
    a. dinner
    b. a concert
    c. a dancing party

(   ) 3. Li You says tomorrow evening she will be _____.
    a. at a restaurant
    b. at a concert
    c. a meeting

65

II. Speaking Exercises

Section One (Answer the questions in Chinese based on the texts)

A. Dialogue I
1. How did Wang Peng know Li You? Please explain.
2. Do you think that Wang Peng and Li You like each other? Please explain.
3. What will Wang Peng and Li You do this weekend?
4. Do you think that Li You wants to see the Chinese movie? Please explain.
5. Do you think that they will be able to see the movie? Please explain.
6. Who else will be going to the movie with them?

B. Dialogue II
1. How did Bai Jianming meet Li You? Please explain.
2. How did Bai Jianming know Li You's phone number?
3. Can Li You go out with Bai Jianming next weekend after her exam? Please explain.
4. Would Li You be willing to go out with Bai Jianming if she is free? Please explain.

Section Two

A. You met someone at a dance last weekend. You like that person very much. Call that person and invite him/her to have dinner first and then go to a movie. When you make the phone call tell him/her that you danced with him/her last weekend.

B. Someone you don't like is calling you and asking you for a date. Try to decline his/her invitation politely by telling him/her that you will be busy for the next two weekends.

C. Tell your friend that you went to see an excellent opera. The tickets were very difficult to get, but you were able to get the tickets eventually by going through a lot of trouble.

D. Tell a story based on the picture below.

III. Reading Comprehension

Section One (Answer the question about the dialogues)

A. Dialogue I

1. 你覺得李友喜歡王朋嗎？為什麼？

2. 《活著》的戲票容易買嗎？你怎麼知道？

3. 李友不想看《活著》，對不對？

4. 一共有幾個人一起去看電影？

B. Dialogue II

1. 白健明會跳舞嗎？你怎麼知道？

2. 白健明為什麼打電話給李友？

3. 這幾個週末，李友要做什麼？

4. 你覺得李友喜歡白健明嗎？為什麼？

Section Two

A. Read the following passage and answer the questions.(True/False)

> 小謝跟小馬認識已經快半年了，他們都在同一班學日文。小馬去過日本，日文說得比小謝好，所以他常常幫助小謝練習說日文。小馬不太會做飯，週末的時候，小謝常常請小馬到她家去吃飯，一起說日文，也一起看日文的錄像。小馬覺得他越來越喜歡小謝。小謝覺得小馬是一個很好的人，又聰明，又用功，還很喜歡幫助別的同學。這個星期小謝的爸爸媽媽要來看她，她想把小馬介紹給他們。

(　　) 1. 小謝跟小馬是同班同學。

(　　) 2. 小謝的日文說得沒有小馬好。

(　　) 3. 週末的時候, 小謝常常請小馬到外頭去吃飯。

(　　) 4. 小謝對小馬的印象很好。

(　　) 5. 小謝的爸爸媽媽已經見過小馬了。

B. Read the following passage and answer the questions.(True/False)

> 在中國，很多女孩找對象，喜歡找比自己高，而且年紀比自己大的男孩。以前有的地方同姓的人不能結婚。在台灣，有些男人不喜歡跟比自己小三歲、六歲或者九歲的人結婚，因為很多人說如果這樣，結婚以後不會快樂。

(　　) 1. 中國女孩喜歡自己比對象長得高.

(　　) 2. 中國女孩喜歡找年紀比自己小的男孩。

(　　) 3. 以前姓王的不能跟姓王的結婚。

(　　) 4. 台灣男人都不跟比自己小三歲、六歲、或九歲的女人結婚。

IV. Writing and Grammar Exercises

Section One

A. Make sentences using the given phrases.

      Example: 玩　高興

         ===> 昨天我們玩得很高興。

1. 打球　　　累

2. 跳舞　　　高興

3. 忙　　　　沒有時間睡覺

4. 笑　　　　肚子疼了

5. 看書　　　忘了時間

B. Make "topic-comment" sentences with the given topics.

      Example: 學中文：

        ===>學中文，我覺得很有意思。

1. 中文錄像：

2. 健康保險：

3. 生日舞會：

4. 住在宿舍裏：

5. 在飯館吃飯：

6. 吃藥打針：

C. Complete the following sentences by selecting from the potential complements listed
    below.

   買不到，聽不到，吃不到，想不到，想不起來，吃不(習)慣，看不懂，聽不懂

1. 她媽媽來美國才半年，_____。
   (not used to American food)

2. 我的中文不太好，_____。
   (unable to understand Chinese movies)

3. 那個書店只有中文書和英文書，_____。
   (unable to buy Japanese books)

4. 老師說話說得太快，_____。(unable to understand)

5. 李友的電話號碼，_____。(unable to recall)

D. Complete the following sentences with 就.

1. 今天看電影的人真少，_____。

2. 我爸爸媽媽說他們要一起開車來看我，_____。

3. 他不會打球，不會唱歌，不會跳舞，_____。

4. 今天來參加小林的生日舞會的人我都不認識，_____。

E. Following the model, combine each pair of the sentences into one.

    Example: 我昨天看了一個電影。那個電影很有意思。

    ===> 我昨天看的那個電影很有意思。

1. 我朋友給我買了一件衣服。那件衣服很合適。

2. 我上個星期天認識了一個朋友。那個朋友很喜歡看歌劇。

3. 我的表姐前天吃了一種藥。那種藥沒有用。

4. 她的男朋友送了她一件襯衫。那件襯衫不便宜。

5. 他的女朋友買了一盤錄音帶。那盤錄音帶很好聽。

6. 他昨天在圖書館借了一本書。那本書是新的。

F. Translate the time expressions below.

1. next week:

2. the day after tomorrow:

3. the month after next:

4. the week before last:

5. the year after next:

6. the semester after next:

G. Complete the following sentences by using the duplicate forms of the following verbs
    or verb phrases.

慶祝，整理，練習，聽錄音，打掃房子，打球

1. 功課做完了，_____，你想一起去嗎？

2. 老師說我_____，中文就會說得更好。

3. 下個星期六是我媽媽五十歲生日，_____。

4. 今天晚上有很多朋友來我家玩，我得先_____。

5. 我的中文說得還不夠好，老師說＿＿＿＿＿＿＿＿＿＿＿＿＿＿＿＿＿＿＿。

6. 你的床上有書，地上也有書，你應該＿＿＿＿＿＿＿＿＿＿＿＿＿＿＿＿＿＿＿。

H. Translate the following into Chinese.

1. He finished his homework long time ago. He is watching T.V. now.（早就）

2. I have wanted to watch that video for a long time.（早就）

3. Look at it carefully. It is my book, not yours. (duplication of verb)

4. Forget It. I know you two won't help me.（算了吧，你倆）

5. The day after tomorrow I will go to see an opera with the girl who often helps me.

6. I would like to try it. (reduplication of verb)

7. I am the only one who is going to China to travel.（就）

8. I have not been to New York. (Topic-comment sentence)

9. My father has a very good impression of my boyfriend.

10. He bought too much fruit. We can't eat it all. (complement of potential)

11. If you don't have time to help me clean the house, then forget it. (要是，就算了)

12. *A:* After the examination, let's have a big celebration. (好好兒, verb duplication)

    B: OK. It's a deal.

Section Two

A. Write a letter to your Chinese friend whom you met last weekend at a birthday party. Tell her/him that you enjoyed dancing with her/him very much, and that you really had a great time at the party. There will be an opera at your school next Friday, and you would like to invite her/him to the opera. Before going to the opera, you would like to have dinner with her/him.

B. Write a couple of paragraphs describing what you did for the past three weekends. You might want to include things such as studying, doing household chores, etc.

Lesson Eighteen   Renting an Apartment

I. Listening Comprehension

Section One (Listen to the tape for the textbook)

A. Narrative (True/False)

(   ) 1. Wang Peng has been living in the dorm for a week so far.
(   ) 2. Wang Peng feels that the dorm is too noisy, and that his room is not big enough.
(   ) 3. It only took Wang Peng two days to find an apartment.
(   ) 4. The apartment is right next to the university. It is very convenient.
(   ) 5. The apartment is furnished, and has its own kitchen too.

B. Dialogue (True/False)

(   ) 1. The apartment is a studio.
(   ) 2. The apartment has a study with a desk and bookcases.
(   ) 3. The rent is $450.00 per month including utilities.
(   ) 4. Pets are not allowed in the apartment.
(   ) 5. Wang Peng decided not to rent the apartment because it is too expensive.

Section Two (Listen to the tape for the workbook)

A. Narrative (True/False)

(   ) 1. In China, all college students live in student dorms.
(   ) 2. All American colleges have student dorms, but not all students live in the dorms.
(   ) 3. Chinese students live in dorms because it is very quiet there.

B. Dialogue (Multiple choice)

(   ) 1. Wang Peng says his apartment is _____.
     a. quiet and convenient but not well furnished
     b. quiet and well furnished but not convenient
     c. quiet and convenient but the kitchen is a bit too small

(   ) 2. It is most likely that tomorrow Wang Peng will eat _____.
     a. in a Chinese restaurant
     b. in his own apartment
     c. in the student dorm where he used to live

(   ) 3. Wang Peng promised to invite the girl _____.
     a. to eat in a restaurant
     b. to a dinner cooked by himself
     c. to cook dinner for him in his apartment

(   ) 4. Which of the following statements can most reasonably be concluded from the dialogue?
     a. Wang Peng is not a good cook yet.
     b. Wang Peng does not want to cook.
     c. The girl is going to teach Wang Peng how to cook.

II. Speaking Exercises

Section One (Answer the questions in Chinese based on the texts)

A. Narrative
1. How long has Wang Peng been living in the dorm?
2. Why does Wang Peng wish to move out?
3. How long has Wang Peng been looking for an apartment?
4. How did Wang Peng learn about that apartment?
5. Can you describe that apartment?

B. Dialogue
1. How did Wang Peng start his phone call to the landlord? How did the landlord respond to him?
2. What did the landlord say about the furniture in that apartment?
3. What is the $450.00 for? Please explain.
4. Can you keep your dog in the apartment? Why?

Section Two

A. Describe the place you live in Chinese. Don't forget to mention the furniture!

B. You don't like the house you are currently living in, so you are making phone calls to look for a new one. Ask about the rent, environment, and facilities.

C. Tell a story based on the picture below.

III. Reading Comprehension

Section One (Answer the questions about the dialogues)

A. Narrative

1. 王朋現在住在哪兒？住了多久了？

2. 王朋為什麼要找公寓？

3. 王朋怎麼找公寓？

4. 王朋覺得那套公寓方便嗎？合適嗎？為什麼？

B. Dialogue II

1. 那個公寓有幾個臥室？

2. 那個公寓有什麼傢俱？

3. 王朋是不是一個很吵的人？你怎麼知道？

4. 如果你要租那套公寓，你得付四百五十元押金，對不對？

5. 你可以在公寓養狗嗎？為什麼？

Section Two

A. Read the following passage and answer the questions. (True/False)

小馬現在住在學生宿舍，他一個人住一個房間。宿舍裏有餐廳、圖書室、電腦室，還有洗衣房，非常方便。小馬不太會做飯，很喜歡認識新朋友，所以他很喜歡住宿舍。他聽說在校外租房子比住宿舍便宜，但是得跟別人一起住，還得自己做飯。小馬雖然想住便宜的房子，但是不想自己做飯，所以他現在還不知道他下學期是不是應該搬出去住。

(   ) 1. 小馬有自己的房間。

(   ) 2. 小馬不喜歡住宿舍。

(   ) 3. 小馬覺得在餐廳吃飯很方便。

(   ) 4. 在校外租房子比住學校宿舍便宜。

(   ) 5. 小馬下學期要搬到校外去住。

B. Read the following passage and answer the questions. (True/False)

在台灣租房子要付一個月的房租當押金。以後要是想搬走，必須在搬家前一個月讓房東知道，要不然押金就拿不回來了。另外，搬家的時候也得把房子打掃乾淨。

(   ) 1. 在台灣租房子得付押金。

(   ) 2. 在台灣租房子一次得住一年，要不然押金就拿不回來。

(   ) 3. 搬家的時候房東會幫你打掃房子。

IV. Writing and Grammar Exercises

Section One

A. Complete the following short dialogues.

1. *A:* 你聽錄音聽了幾個鐘頭了？

   B: _____ 。

2. *A:* _____ 。

   B: 我學中文學了八個月了。

3. *A:* 你上大學上了多久了？

   B: _____ 。

B. Rewrite the following sentences using the structure "連...都/也..."
1. 他忘了女朋友的生日。

2. 我最近很忙，沒有時間睡覺。

3. 他中文學得很好，看得懂中文小說。

4. 這個房間很小，放不下一張書桌。

5. 這個字很難，老師不會寫。

C. Follow the model, and rewrite the following sentences using the structure "question word + 都."

Example: *A:* 他常常看錄像嗎？

　　　　　　B: 他什麼錄像都不看。

1. *A:* 你的朋友會唱什麼歌？

　　B: _____。

2. *A:* 除了聽音樂以外，今天晚上你還想做什麼？

　　B: _____。

3. *A:* 這個孩子喜歡看什麼書？

　　B: _____。

4. *A:* 你餓了吧，想吃什麼？

　　B: 我肚子疼，_____。

D. Complete the following dialogue.

A: 你在這個公寓住了多久了？(more than a year)

B:

A: 房租每個月多少錢？(six hundred)

B:

A: 押金多少錢？(one thousand)

B:

A: 你可以在你的公寓裏養動物嗎？(not allowed)

B:

A: 你的公寓帶傢俱嗎？(not furnished)

B:

A: 要是你想找一個可以養動物和帶傢俱的公寓，我可以幫你看報上的廣告。
(No, thanks. I can read the newspaper myself.)

B:

E. Translate the following into Chinese.

1. He has slept for over twenty hours (but less than 30). (V+了+Nu+M+Time + 了，多)

2. How can we study Lesson Ten when we haven't studied Lesson Nine yet? (連...都，怎麼)

3. He didn't like any of the apartments. (interrogative pronoun with 都)

4. He reads all kinds of advertisements. (什麼...都)

5. I have a little over ten dollars (less than eleven).

6. You'd better not rent that apartment because it is not furnished. (最好)

7. There is a sofa in the living room. In addition, there are a bookshelf and a desk in the living room. (有，還有)

8. There are two single beds in the bedroom. One is on the left side, and the other is on the right side. (有)

9. The kitchen is too small. There is no room for a dining table and six chairs. (V +不下)

10. Yesterday evening, over twenty people went to see the movie. (多)

11. My apartment is only one mile away from the school. (離)

12. No pets are allowed in this dormitory. (interrogative pronoun with 都, 許)

Section Two

A. Write a letter to your friend asking him/her to find you a one-bedroom apartment near the university. You prefer a furnished apartment under $500.00 per month. You don't mind paying a security deposit, but you do not wish to pay for utilities. Also, since you have a dog, you need to find a place where pets are allowed.

B. You wish to rent out the extra room in your house. Can you write an advertisement for it? Be sure to include the following information:
   -- The room is furnished with a single bed, a desk, two chairs, and two bookshelves
   -- Utilities are included
   -- One month rent required for security deposit
   -- Monthly rent is $250.00
   -- Quiet people preferred

Lesson Nineteen   Post Office

I. Listening Comprehension

Section One (Listen to the tape for the textbook)

A. Dialogue I (True/False)
(   ) 1. The woman wished to mail a letter to Tainan.
(   ) 2. The woman decided to send the letter by express mail.
(   ) 3. The postage for the express mail was fourteen dollars.
(   ) 4. In addition to mailing the letter, the woman also bought some stamps.
(   ) 5. A postcard costs three dollars.

B. Dialogue II (True/False)
(   ) 1. The man is seeking advice from the woman.
(   ) 2. The man used to send flowers to Zhang Yiwen on her birthday.
(   ) 3. Zhang Yiwen and the man live in the same city.
(   ) 4. The man deposited the check into the bank.

Section Two (Listen to the tape for the workbook)

A. Dialogue (Multiple choice)
(   ) 1. How many days does it usually take for a letter to travel from here to New York?
        a. At least three days.
        b. At least five days.
        c. At least a week.

(   ) 2. Based on the dialogue, which of the following statements is true?
        a. If the man's brother sends him a letter from New York, his brother will
           get his reply at least two weeks later.
        b. If the man's brother writes to somebody in New York, he will get the reply
           at least seven days later.
        c. If the man writes to his brother in New York, he will get his reply after
           six or seven days at the earliest.

(   ) 3. Judging from the context, the word "huíxìn" means _____.
        a. a letter returned to the sender
        b. a letter sent in reply
        c. a letter to one's relative

(   ) 4. Last Monday the man wrote a letter to _____.
        a. himself for fun
        b. the postmaster
        c. his brother

(   ) 5. Last Wednesday the man received a letter written by _____.
   - a. himself
   - b. his brother
   - c. the postmaster

B. Narrative (True/False)

(   ) 1. According to the passage, Wang Peng did not have a credit card when he was in China.

(   ) 2. Wang Peng heard from his friends that many people in China and Taiwan are starting to use credit cards.

(   ) 3. Wang Peng uses his credit card only in restaurants.

II. Speaking Exercises

Section One (Answer the questions in Chinese based on the dialogues)

A. Dialogue I

1. How long does it take to send a letter from Taipei to Tainan by regular mail? How about express mail?
2. Is the woman sending the letter by regular mail or express mail? Why?
3. How much extra will it cost if the woman wants to send the letter by registered mail?
4. Did the woman buy anything else besides the stamps?
5. What is the $141.00 dollars for? Please explain.

B. Dialogue II

1. What did the man give Zhang Yiwen for her birthday in the past?
2. What did the woman suggest that the man buy for Zhang Yiwen's birthday? Why?
3. How will the man have the present delivered to Zhang Yiwen?
4. Who sent the man a check? Can he deposit it in the post office?
5. What currency does the post office accept?

Section Two

A. You are in a post office in Taiwan and would like to send a very important letter to your parents in New York. Find out how many days it takes to send an air mail letter to New York, and how much the postage costs. Also find out how much extra you need to pay if you want to send the letter by registered mail.

B. You go to a post office in Beijing to buy stamps and send something, but you run into some problems. Ask the clerk to help you.

III. Reading Exercises

Section I

A. Dialogue I

1. 留學生現在在哪兒？她要寄信到哪兒？

2. 寄平信要幾天？寄快信呢？

3. 爲什麼留學生要寄掛號快信？

4. 她寄一封掛號快信一共要多少錢？

5. 除了寄信以外，留學生在郵局還買別的東西了嗎？

6. 留學生花了多少錢買明信片？

7. 十張郵票要多少錢？

B. Dialogue II

1. 下個月是誰的生日？

2. 白先生以前送過花給張意文嗎？你怎麼知道？

3. 白先生住在上海嗎？你怎麼知道？

4. 從北京可以送花到上海嗎？怎麼送？

5. 白先生把一張美金支票存在郵局裏，對不對？爲什麼？

Section Two

A. Read the passage below and answer the questions. (True/False)

> 小張從中國來美國念書已經半年了，他很想念他在北京的家人，一個星期寫一封信回家。他很想跟家裏的人聊天，可是電話費太貴，每分鐘要一塊多，所以他一個半月才往家裏打一次電話。每次打電話，爸爸媽媽都不讓他説得太久，因爲不想讓他花太多錢。

(   ) 1. 小張是中國人。

(   ) 2. 小張一個月寫四封信回家。

(   ) 3. 從來美國到現在，小張已經往家裏打過十二次電話了。

(   ) 4. 因爲不常打電話，小張每次打電話都跟家裏的人聊很久。

B. Read the passage below and answer the questions. (True/False)

> 以前小馬出去旅行的時候，不買旅行支票，也沒有信用卡，所以他帶很多現金。有一次，他到日本去玩，離開美國以前，到銀行去拿了兩千塊美金的現金。到東京的第二天，他的錢就丟了。他在日本因爲沒有錢，所以玩得一點都不高興。小馬想以後出門，一定要買旅行支票，現金只帶一點就可以了。

(   ) 1. 小馬以前出去旅行用旅行支票。

(   ) 2. 他去日本以前，在美國換了一些日元。

(   ) 3. 他丟的錢，很快就找到了。

(   ) 4. 小馬以後到別的地方旅行，不會帶很多現金。

IV. Writing and Grammar Exercises

Section One

A. Answer the following questions.

1. *A:* 從學校寄信到你家要多少天？

   B: _____ 。

2. *A:* 從紐約開車到你家要多久？

   B: _____ 。

3. *A:* 從你的宿舍到圖書館遠不遠？怎麼走？

   B: _____ 。

4. *A:* 從開始學中文到現在，你學了多少漢字了？

   B: _____ 。

B. Complete the following short conversations:

1. *A:* 一張明信片_____？我想買五張。

   B: _____ 兩塊錢，五張一共 _____ 。

2. *A:* 除了五張明信片，我還要買十張郵票，一張 _____ ？

   B: _____ 三塊錢。

3. *A:* _____ ？

   B: _____ 十塊錢，十張_____ 。

   一共 _____ 。

C. Answer the following questions with approximate numerals.
    Example: 你多久去一次圖書館？

         ===>我每兩、三天去一次圖書館。

1. 你多久給你媽媽打一次電話？

2. 你們常常幾個人一起出去吃飯？

3. 十九歲的學生可能上大學幾年級？

4. 你一個月花多少錢？

D. Following the model, rewrite the following sentences using the expression
    "除了...都".
       Example: 今天晚上我只想看報，不想做別的事。

          ===> 今天晚上除了看報以外，別的事我都不想做。

1. 我只喝茶，不喝別的。

2. 住宿舍我就怕吵，別的都不怕。

3. 只有一個同學沒預習課文，別的同學都預習了。

4. 我們都去過北京，可是我弟弟還沒有去過北京。

E. Fill in the blanks with 還 or 都 .

1. 你週末除了跳舞以外，_____喜歡做什麼？

2. 除了小張以外，我們_____不吃牛肉。

3. 老王除了報紙以外，什麼_____不看。

4. 我的房間裏除了一張床以外，什麼_____沒有。

5. 除了書桌以外，她_____買了兩個書架。

6. 除了首飾以外，他_____常常給女朋友送花。

F. Complete the following sentences with 越...越....

Example: 我覺得房子越大越好。 (the bigger the better)

1. 他很喜歡買衣服，他告訴我_____。
   (the more the better)

2. 學生都說考試_____。
   (the easier the better)

3. 這種水果_____。
   (the bigger the tastier)

4. 這種首飾_____。
   (the smaller the more expensive)

G. Translate the following into Chinese:

1. How long does it take to send a letter by regular mail from Beijing to New York?
   (從...到)

2. I'd like to buy five bottles of fruit juice. How much for each? (一...多少錢)

3. It's one dollar and twenty cents for each bottle. Altogether it's six dollars. (一共)

4. This kind of pants is very expensive. They cost fifty or sixty dollars a pair.
   (approximate numerals)

5. The more money a bank has, the better. (越...越...)

6. I can do everything except cook. (除了...以外，都)

7. In addition to playing the piano, I also like to travel and play ball. (除了...還)

8. She has been driving faster and faster recently. (越...越...)

9. My father said that I cannot go traveling in China unless I learn Chinese well first.
   (先...才)

10. The teacher asks us to listen to the tapes two or three hours everyday.
    (approximate numerals)

11. Her boyfriend gave her a bunch of flowers as her birthday present. (當)

12. If I send by express mail, when can my friend receive this letter?

Section Two

A. Write a letter to your friend in Taiwan to find out how the post office works there.
    Ask him/her the cost for the following:
    -- Sending a letter by regular mail from one city to another in Taiwan.
    -- Sending a letter by air mail from Taiwan to the United States.
    -- A postcard.
    -- Sending a letter by registered mail from one city to another city in Taiwan.

B. Write a letter to your Chinese friend explaining that it normally takes 2 to 3 days to send a letter from New York to Boston. If you want the letter to get there as soon as possible, you should send it through express mail which only takes one day. Also, tell your friend that while one can deposit money at the post office in China, one cannot do it in the United States. Neither do post offices in the United States sell postcards.

Lesson Twenty   Sports

I. Listening Comprehension

Section One (Listen to the tape for the textbook)

A. Dialogue I (True/False)
(   ) 1. The man eats a lot, but he also exercises a lot.
(   ) 2. The woman suggests that the man exercise at least three hours each week.
(   ) 3. The man did not jog in the past two years.
(   ) 4. The man prefers to jog in the winter rather than in the summer.
(   ) 5. The man thinks that playing basketball is a lot of trouble.
(   ) 6. The man likes to swim because he can do it by himself.

B. Dialogue II (True/False)
(   ) 1. Siwen came to the States to go to college.
(   ) 2. Siwen watches TV every day because he wants to improve his English.
(   ) 3. The woman likes to watch football.
(   ) 4. They are watching a soccer match on the TV.

Section Two (Listen to the tape for the workbook)

A. Dialogue (Multiple choice)
(   ) 1. What sports are mentioned in the dialogue?
        a. Basketball, football, and swimming.
        b. Football, tennis, and swimming.
        c. Basketball, tennis, and swimming.
        d. Football, swimming, and table tennis.

(   ) 2. Why did the man quit playing tennis?
        a. It is too hot to play tennis in the summer.
        b. He feels very tired after playing it.
        c. It is too costly for him.
        d. He thinks that tennis is not as exciting as basketball.

(   ) 3. Which of the statements is most likely to be true?
        a. The man loves several kinds of sports.
        b. The man loves basketball more than swimming.
        c. The man has failed to persevere in any of the sports.
        d. The man hates basketball, but loves tennis.

(   ) 4. What sport (or sports) is the man engaged in right now?
        a. Swimming   b. No sport at all
        c. Football   d. Tennis and basketball

B. Narrative (True/False)

(   ) 1. Wang Peng started to like American football as soon as he came to the U.S.
(   ) 2. Wang Peng used to think that American football was too dangerous.
(   ) 3. Wang Peng likes basketball better than American football.
(   ) 4. Wang Peng never watches American football games on TV.

II. Speaking Exercises

Section One (Answer the questions in Chinese based on the dialogues)

A. Dialogue I
1. What did the man say about his body?
2. How did the woman respond to the man?
3. What did the woman suggest the man do to lose weight?
4. What sport did the man decide to do?

B. Dialogue II
1. Who is Siwen? Why did Siwen come to the States?
2. Why does Siwen watch TV for two hours every day?
3. What is playing on channel 6?
4. Does the man like to watch football? Please explain.
5. Why did the woman tell the man not to worry about the football players?

Section Two

A. Among the sports listed below, which one do you like the most? Which one do you like the least? Why?
    --Tennis, basketball, soccer, jogging, swimming, football, etc.

B. Explain to your Chinese friend the differences between soccer and football.

C. Describe the two sports below. Do point out their differences.

A   B

III. Reading Exercises

Section I

A. Dialogue I

1. 為什麼老李的肚子越來越大？

2. 小林說肚子怎麼可以小一點兒？

3. 老李為什麼說跑步很難受？

4. 老李為什麼不想打網球？

5. 老李為什麼說打籃球很麻煩？

6. 老李喜歡游泳嗎？為什麼？

7. 你想老李會更胖嗎？為什麼？

B. Dialogue II

1. 思文來美國做什麼？

2. 思文為什麼每天看電視？

3. 思文喜歡看美式足球嗎？你是怎麼知道的？

4. 國際足球跟美式足球有什麼不同？

5. 思文喜歡看美式足球賽嗎？你是怎麼知道的？

Section Two

A. Read the passage below and answer the questions. (True/False)

> 台灣人很喜歡看棒球比賽，因為十幾年前台灣的棒球隊打得很好，常常得到世界冠軍。那個時候常常在美國比賽，因為美國跟台灣有十幾個小時的時差，所以為了看球賽，台灣人常常半夜起來看電視。

(　　) 1. 台灣的棒球隊沒有得到過世界冠軍。

(　　) 2. 美國是白天的時候，台灣是晚上。

(　　) 3. 以前台灣人看棒球賽的時候，連覺都可以不睡。

B. Read the passage below and answer the questions. (True/False)

> 中國的年輕人跟老年人都喜歡運動。很多年輕人不但喜歡打乒乓球，而且打得很好。打乒乓球跟打籃球不一樣，個子不必太高，所以是一種很適合中國人的運動。中國的老年人喜歡早上到公園去打太極拳，打完太極拳以後，他們常常先跟朋友聊一會天兒再回家。

(　　) 1. 中國很多的年輕人很會打乒乓球。

(　　) 2. 打乒乓球的人個子越高越好。

(　　) 3. 每天早上公園裏有很多老年人在打太極拳。

(　　) 4. 老年人打完太極拳以後，馬上回家。

IV. Writing and Grammar Exercises

Section One

A. Complete the following sentences using the negative forms.

Example: 我餓死了，<u>已經（有）兩天沒吃飯了</u>。
         (have not eaten for two days)

1. 王朋去哪兒了？＿＿＿＿＿＿＿＿＿＿＿＿＿＿＿＿＿＿＿＿＿＿＿＿＿。
  (have not seen him for two weeks)

2. *A:* 你學過日文嗎？
  B: 學過，學過三年。
  A: 你可以教我嗎？
  B: 不行，＿＿＿＿＿＿＿＿＿＿＿＿＿＿＿＿＿＿＿＿＿，已經忘了。
      (have not spoken Japanese for a long time)

3. 小白忙極了，＿＿＿＿＿＿＿＿＿＿＿＿＿＿＿＿＿＿＿＿＿＿＿。
  (has not called his mother for two months)

4. 小張很想去中國飯館，因為＿＿＿＿＿＿＿＿＿＿＿＿＿＿＿＿＿＿＿。
  (has not eaten Chinese food for half a year)

5. 他的身體越來越不好，因為＿＿＿＿＿＿＿＿＿＿＿＿＿＿＿＿＿＿。
  (has not exercised for more than a year)

B. Fill in the blanks with "住下去, 說下去, 熱下去, 跳下去, 學下去. "

1. 天氣太熱了，真受不了，再＿＿＿＿＿＿＿＿＿＿＿＿＿，我就要熱死了。

2. 這個宿舍太吵，我不想＿＿＿＿＿＿＿＿＿＿＿＿＿＿＿＿＿＿＿＿了。

3. 雖然中文很難，但是我還是想＿＿＿＿＿＿＿＿＿＿＿＿＿＿＿＿。

4. 你唱歌唱得太難聽了, 別＿＿＿＿＿＿＿＿＿＿＿＿＿＿＿＿了。

5. 我跳舞已經跳了五個小時了, 再＿＿＿＿＿＿＿＿＿＿＿＿＿, 就要累死了。

C. Rewrite the following sentences using "起來. "

Example: 她一回家就開始聽錄音。

===> 她一回家就聽起錄音來。

1. 他剛上課，頭就開始疼了。

2. 現在才三月，天氣就開始熱了。

3. 他吃得很多，又不運動，開始胖了。

4. 他們一考完試，就開始打球。

D. Answer the following questions using "被. "

Example: A: 請問，你們這間房子出租嗎？ (rented by someone, 租)

B: 對不起，房子已經被人租去了。

1. A: 你可以把新買的書借我看看嗎？ (borrowed by someone, 借)

B: 對不起，_____ 。

2. A: 我的網球拍怎麼壞了？ (ruined by younger brother, 打)

B: 你的網球拍_____ 。

3. A: 媽媽，再給我一些錢吧。 (taken away by older brother, 拿)

B: 我昨天剛給你兩百塊，你都花了？

A: 沒有，_____ 。

4. A: 你的手怎麼了？ (crushed, 壓)

B: 我的手受傷了，是昨天足球比賽的時候_____ 。

D. Fill in the blanks with "起來" and "下去."

　　昨天下午我在學校看到我的小學同學老田，我們聊了＿＿＿＿＿＿。我看他比以前瘦了，就問他爲什麼。他告訴我，他以前不太忙，很舒服，可是最近開始考試了，所以忙＿＿＿＿＿了。我告訴他，他不能再瘦＿＿＿＿＿了，要多注意自己的身體健康。他說，他在宿舍住很不習慣。我說，住宿舍對學英文有好處，你還是住＿＿＿＿＿吧，幾個月以後你的英文就會好＿＿＿＿＿了。

E. Answer the following questions.

1. 你多長時間看一次電影？

2. 你多長時間運動一次？每次運動多久？

3. 你多長時間去一次中國飯館？

4. 你多長時間上一次銀行？

5. 你多久沒看到你的爸爸了？

6. 你多久沒打電話給你的好朋友了？

7. 你多久沒看電視了？

8. 你多久沒寫信了？

F. Translate the following into Chinese.

1. I haven't been to school for a week. (没. . . 了)

2. My younger brother has bought three tennis rackets so far this year. (了. . . 了)

3. As soon as he finished his meal, he started to watch TV. (一. . . 就, 起來)

4. Please stop saying that. I feel it hard to bear. (下去, 難受)

5. I have not had a bath for three days. It's very uncomfortable. (duration + 了)

6. I have been playing tennis for more than ten years. (duration + 了)

7. She jogs 40 minutes everyday. (duration)

8. Many football players have been hurt by being crushed. (被)

9. In order to improve his listening comprehension, he listens to recordings two hours a day. (為了)

10. I don't like to watch (American) football because I can't tell who is winning and who is losing.

Section Two

A. Describe the exercises that you do to stay fit. How often do you exercise? And for how long each time?

B. Write a letter to your Chinese friend telling him/her what sports are popular in the States. Describe your personal feelings toward those sports.

Lesson Twenty-One   Travel

I. Listening Comprehension

Section One (Listen to the tape for the textbook)

A. Dialogue I (True/False)
(   ) 1. The woman is going to Taiwan in one month.
(   ) 2. The man has never been to Taiwan before.
(   ) 3. The man will leave for Taiwan in the middle of June.
(   ) 4. The man has already purchased the plane ticket.
(   ) 5. Both Northwest Airlines and China Airlines are having a sale.

B. Dialogue II (Multiple choice)
(   ) 1. What does the man want to buy?
        a. A one-way ticket to Beijing.
        b. A round-trip ticket to Beijing.
        c. A one way ticket to Washington, D.C.
        d. A round-trip ticket to Washington, D.C.
(   ) 2. Where does the man's trip begin?
        a. Beijing.
        b. Washington, D.C.
        c. Chicago.
        d. Los Angeles.
(   ) 3. Where will the man spend a night during his trip?
        a. Chicago.
        b. Los Angeles.
        c. Seoul.
        d. Hong Kong.
(   ) 4. What airline has the lowest fare?
        a. Air China.
        b. Northwest Airlines.
        c. Korean Airlines.
        d. US Air.
(   ) 5. What will happen next week?
        a. There will be a sale.
        b. The price will go up.
        c. The ticket will be issued.
        d. The deposit will be returned.

Section Two (Listen to the tape for the workbook)

A. Dialogue (Multiple choice)
(   ) 1. If you fly round trip with Northwest Airlines from New York to Beijing, how much will it cost you, according to the dialogue?
        a. $1,020   b. $1,200   c. $1,380   d. $1,400

(   ) 2. Why didn't the man want to fly Korean Airlines? Because of the _____.
        a. price   b. aircraft   c. connection d. service
(   ) 3. How long did the man plan to stay in Beijing?
        a. one week b. two weeks c. three weeks d. one month
(   ) 4. Why did the man decide not to order the ticket in the end?
        a. He had no credit card.
        b. He did not want to give his credit card number.
        c. He did not want to write a check.
        d. He had not got his visa yet.

B. Narrative (True/False)
(   ) 1. Little Gao went to Chicago for a visit two years ago, but has never been to New
        York.
(   ) 2. Little Gao plans to go to New York two or three weeks after the semester ends.
(   ) 3. According to the passage, the price of the airline ticket is at least twice as much
        as that of the bus ticket.
(   ) 4. According to the passage, it takes about an hour to get a bus ticket but twenty-
        four hours to get a plane ticket.

II. Speaking Exercises

Section One (Answer the questions in Chinese based on the dialogues)

A. Dialogue I
1. What does the man intend to do in Taiwan?
2. What advice did the woman give to the man concerning his trip to Taiwan?
3. Did the man have any idea about buying airline tickets? Has he bought a ticket yet?
4. Why did the woman say that her brother can help the man?

B. Dialogue II
1. Why did the man call the travel agency?
2. How much is a round-trip ticket to Beijing?
3. What airline does the man prefer?
4. What will the man's itinerary be if he flies Korean Airlines to Beijing?
5. What did the woman say when the man asked her about direct flight to Beijing?
6. What is the final advice that the woman gave to the man?

Section Two

A. Situational Conversation: Find a partner to be your travel agent. You call the agent
    to book a plane ticket. You are going to Taipei at the end of August. You would like
    to leave on a Monday and return on a Saturday. Select the best flight based on price
    and dates. Your partner will try to be as helpful as possible.

B. Talk about your most enjoyable trip or the most recent one.

III. Reading Exercises

Section One

A. Dialogue I

1. 放假的時候小白打算到哪裏去？

2. 小錢計劃到台灣去做什麼？

3. 小錢什麼時候要到台灣去？

4. 去台灣以前，小錢得做哪些事？

5. 昨天小錢看報了嗎？你怎麼知道？

6. 為什麼小白要小錢把他的旅行日程告訴他？

7. 為什麼小白要小錢請他吃飯？

B. Dialogue II

1. 王朋給哪家旅行社打電話？

2. 王朋為什麼給旅行社打電話？

3. 王朋想買哪家航空公司的機票？

4. 要是王朋坐韓航的飛機，得在什麼地方住一個晚上？

5. 哪幾家航空公司有從洛杉磯直飛北京的班機？

6. 為什麼旅行社的職員要王朋早一點訂票？

7. 西北航空公司的機票最便宜，對不對？

Section Two

A. Read the passage below and answer the questions. (True/False)

台北有很多美國人，他們有的是到台灣去旅行，有的是去學中文，有的是去教英文。也有很多人一邊教英文，一邊學中文，有空的時候就到各地去旅行。幾年前，台北有很多人想跟美國人學英文，所以教英文的工作不太難找。可是現在那裏的外國人越來越多，所以教英文的工作越來越難找了。還有外國人必須有工作證才能在台灣工作，要不然是不合法的。

( ) 1. 在台北的美國人都有工作。

( ) 2. 有的美國人到台灣只想去旅行。

( ) 3. 有很多台北人想跟美國人學英文。

( ) 4. 現在外國人在台北找教英文的工作不太難。

( ) 5. 外國人要有工作證才可以在台灣教英文。

B. Read the passage below and answer the questions. (True/False)

小白在加州大學念書，放假的時候他常常跟朋友到各地去玩。因為坐飛機太貴，所以他很少坐飛機。他最喜歡開車到各州的國家公園去看看，有的國家公園，他已經去過兩、三次了。出去旅行的時候他很少住旅館，多半是在公園露營，因為只要付一點錢，就可以在露營的地方住，那裏也有洗澡間和廁所，很便宜。每次出去玩，他都租車，因為他的車是舊車，不太適合長途旅行。而且租的車要是有了問題，可以打電話請租車公司來換車，比開自己的車方便得多。

( ) 1. 小白在加州上學。

( ) 2. 小白放假的時候喜歡一個人去旅行。

( ) 3. 小白旅行的時候常常坐飛機。

( ) 4. 小白旅行的時候不常住旅館，常常露營。

( ) 5. 在公園露營不必付錢。

( ) 6. 露營的地方可以洗澡、上廁所。

（　）7.小白的車不是新車。

（　）8.小白有時候開自己的車去旅行。

（　）9.旅行的時候，租車比開自己的車方便。

IV. Writing and Grammar Exercises

Section One

A. Translate the following into Chinese.

1. to give a discount:

2. 20% off :

3. 15% off:

4. half price:

B. Following the model, rewrite the sentences using the expression "有的. . . 有的. "

   Example:在我家，爸爸和弟弟喜歡吃中國飯，媽媽和妹妹喜歡吃美國飯。

   ===> 在我家，有的人喜歡吃中國飯，有的人喜歡吃美國飯。

1. 在運動場上，有很多人在打球，還有一些人在跑步。

2. 韓國航空公司和中國民航的機票很便宜，西北航空公司的機票很貴。

3. 來美國的中國人，有很多人是來念書的，也有一些人是來工作的。

4. 在圖書館裏，很多人在看書，也有一些人在看報。

5. 週末，我常常出去打球，也常常去看電影。

C. Following the model, answer the questions using interrogative pronouns.

    Example: *A:* 你想租哪個房子？(whichever is cheap)

          B: <u>哪個房子便宜，我就租哪個。</u>

1. *A:* 你姐姐喜歡買什麼衣服？(whatever is expensive)

    B: _____ 。

2. *A:* 你想住哪個公寓？(whichever is the nearest to the school)

    B: _____ 。

3. *A:* 你想看什麼電影？(whatever is interesting)

    B: _____ 。

4. *A:* 我們去哪家飯館？(whichever is good)

    B: _____ 。

D. Following the model, make sentences using the pattern "先...然後."

    Example: 復習   考試

      ===>你應該先復習，然後去考試。

1. 問票價   買機票

2. 預習   上課

3. 看醫生　　吃藥

4. 吃飯　　　　　付錢

5. 去圖書館　　　去活動中心

E. Following the model, describe your itinerary.

Example: 北京 - - ->香港 - - ->洛杉磯 - - ->紐約
===> 先從北京飛到香港，在香港轉機，再從香港飛到洛杉磯，
然後從洛杉磯飛到紐約。

1. 香港 - - ->東京 - - ->芝加哥 - - ->紐約

2. 華盛頓 - - ->芝加哥 - - ->洛杉磯 - - ->台北

3. 波士頓 - - ->東京 - - ->上海 - - ->北京

F. Following the model, make questions and answer them:

      Example: 這條藍褲子十八塊錢，那條黃褲子二十塊。

    ===> *A:*黃褲子比藍褲子貴多少？

        *B:*黃褲子比藍褲子貴兩塊。

1. 從芝加哥到香港，西北航空公司的票價是一千一百五十塊，韓航是一千一百塊。

   A : _____ 。

   B : _____ 。

2. 這個大電腦一千塊錢，那個小電腦兩千多塊。

   A : _____ 。

   B : _____ 。

3. 現在訂機票三百五十塊一張，一個星期以後五百三十塊一張。

   A : _____ 。

   B : _____ 。

4. 我只有一個網球拍，可是我的弟弟有五個。

   A : _____ 。

   B : _____ 。

5. 中國民航的飛機早上八點離開北京，西北航空公司的是下午一點離開北京。

A: _____ 。

B: _____ 。

G. Write the following numbers in Chinese characters.

1. 50,000:

2. 98,764:

3. 30,607:

4. 708,050:

5. 123,456:

6. 6,700,000:

7. 4,000,398:

8. 26,505,489:

9. 700,400,300:

10. 4,386,509,712:

H. Translate the following into Chinese.

1. All bookshelves are on sale, but some are 20% off while others are 30% off. (打折扣, 有的…有的…)

2. I often get sick. Sometimes I have a stomach ache, and sometimes I have a headache. (有的…有的…)

3. We will go to whichever travel agency is good. (哪…哪…)

4. We will have dinner first and then go to a movie. After that we will go dancing. (先…再…然後)

5. The hot-and-sour soup in this restaurant tastes better than that in the other restaurant. And it is also cheaper than the other. (比)

6. He hopes he can take a trip to China in two years. (內)

7. If you pay me now, you can get the plane ticket tomorrow. (要是/ 如果…就…)

8. I want to go to whichever bank you go to. (哪. . .哪. . .)

9. I say whatever I want to. Whoever wants to listen can listen. I am not worried.
    (什麼. . .什麼; 誰. . .誰)

10. Hurry up. You have to come back in an hour. (內)

11. I heard that it is very difficult to get a visa for the month of August. You'd
     better apply for one right away. (最好)

12. The advertisement says that Northwest Airlines tickets are 25% off. (打. . 折)

13. If you send by express mail, it will be there in two days. (要是/ 如果. . 就)

14. Call me if the passport is done. (要是/ 如果. . 就)

Section Two

A. School is almost over. Please write a paragraph describing your ideal travel plan for a two-month summer vacation. Where would you go? Who would you go with? What would you do? How would you travel?

B. Write a letter to your travel agency and ask them to reserve a plane ticket for you when the tickets are on sale next time. You plan to make a trip from Washington, D.C. to Shanghai. If possible, you would like to fly directly from Washington, D.C. to China because you don't like to change planes. Also, tell them that you will fly the airline which offers the lowest fare.

Lesson Twenty-Two   Hometown

I. Listening Comprehension

Section One (Listen to the tape for the textbook)

A. Dialogue I (True/False)
(   ) 1. The man is going to California during the spring break.
(   ) 2. The woman is going to visit her grandparents during the spring break.
(   ) 3. The man has no relatives in the United States.
(   ) 4. The man's aunt lives in San Francisco.
(   ) 5. The woman is from a big city.
(   ) 6. The man has been to the woman's hometown.

B. Dialogue II (True/False)
(   ) 1. The man has lived in the States for more than a year.
(   ) 2. The man is homesick.
(   ) 3. The man's hometown is a political center.
(   ) 4. The man's hometown has four distinctive seasons.
(   ) 5. The man intends to go home during his winter break.

Section Two (Listen to the tape for the workbook)

A. Dialogue (Multiple choice)
(   ) 1. Which of the following is the most reasonable estimate of the distance from
           Wang Peng's hometown to Beijing?
           a. 2 miles   b. 200 miles   c. 50 miles   d. 500 miles

(   ) 2. Wang Peng left his hometown_____ ago.
           a. over two years
           b. exactly two years
           c. about three years
           d. twenty months

(   ) 3. Which of the following statements is most likely to be true?
           a. Wang Peng and his friends used to swim in the river.
           b. Li You once swam in the river near Wang Peng's hometown.
           c. Wang Peng and Li You once swam in the river near Wang Peng's
              hometown.
           d. Wang Peng used to swim in the river alone.

(   ) 4. According to the dialogue, what does Li You think of Wang Peng's hometown?
           a. She thinks it is too close to Beijing.
           b. She loves it and hopes to visit it.
           c. She hopes there will be a swimming pool there.
           d. She thinks it is too far away from the United States.

B. Narrative (True/False)

117

(   ) 1. According to the passage, Los Angeles is a relatively quiet city in spite of the busy traffic.

(   ) 2. Because there are too many vehicles and pedestrians on the streets, life in Los Angeles is not convenient.

(   ) 3. People complain that the weather in Los Angeles is not good because it seldom rains and almost never snows.

(   ) 4. Little Gao's aunt loves Los Angeles and refuses to move away from it.

(   ) 5. Little Gao's aunt loves skiing and would not be bothered too much by cold weather.

II. Speaking Exercises

Section One (Answer the questions in Chinese based on the dialogues)

A. Dialogue I
1. Who is Wang Dezhong? Where does he live? What is he discussing with Li You?
2. What does Li You intend to do during her spring break? How about Wang Dezhong?
3. Could you tell me something about Wang Dezhang's grandparents, his aunt and his uncle?
4. How did Li You describe her hometown?
5. What can you do in Li You's hometown in the four different seasons?

B. Dialogue II
1. How long has Wang Peng been living in the United States?
2. Does Wang Peng like the United States? Please explain.
3. Is Beijing an important city? Why?
4. How did Wang Peng describe Beijing's weather?
5. Why did the woman say that Wang Peng could be the tour guide?

Section Two

A. Describe the geographical settings and climate of your hometown.

B. Talk about your relatives, including what they do and where they live, etc.

C. Describe this picture using what you have learned so far.

III. Reading Exercises

Section One

A. Dialogue I

1. 王德中住在什麼地方？

2. 王德中有什麼親戚住在加州？

3. 李友的老家在舊金山，對不對？

4. 李友老家在一個大城市，對不對？

5. 在李友的老家一年四季可以做哪些事？

6. 王德中去過李友家嗎？ 你怎麼知道？

B. Dialogue II

1. 王朋喜歡美國的生活嗎？

2. 小林去過北京嗎？

3. 王朋的老家是個什麼樣的地方？

4. 北京的氣候怎麼樣？

5. 王朋打算什麼時候回北京？

6. 誰說王朋可以當導遊？為什麼？

Section Two

A. Read the passage and answer the questions (True/False)

> 北京是中國的首都，那裏春、夏、秋、冬氣候不一樣。北京夏天很熱，有的時候很悶，是最不舒服的季節。冬天很冷，但是很好玩，可以到滑冰場去滑冰。春天的北京非常漂亮，公園裏，馬路旁，到處開滿了花，但是因為風很大，沒有秋天舒服。秋天是北京遊客最多的季節，最漂亮的地方是北京西邊的香山，每年一到看紅葉的時候，香山上到處都是人。

(   ) 1. 北京的氣候四季分明。

(   ) 2. 北京的冬天又冷又不好玩，是最不舒服的季節。

(   ) 3. 北京的春天遊客最多。

(   ) 4. 北京的春天比秋天舒服。

(   ) 5. 秋天的時候，香山的遊客很多。

B. Read the passage and answer the questions (True/False)

> 白老師的老家在高雄，高雄是台灣的第二大城市，也是一個海港，有一百多萬人口。高雄的氣候一年四季變化不太大，春天、冬天涼快一點，從來不下雪。夏天很熱，下午常常下大雨，有的時候還有颱風。秋天的天氣跟夏天差不多。白老師有個姐姐住在波士頓附近的一個小鎮，他們已經十多年沒見面了。白老師的姐姐告訴他，美國東部秋天的紅葉非常漂亮，但是可以看紅葉的時間很短，只有兩個星期。白老師打算今年十月中到波士頓去玩半個月，他的姐姐會帶他到各地去看紅葉。

(　) 1. 白老師的老家是一個有一百多萬人口的海港。

(　) 2. 高雄的氣候每個季節都很不一樣。

(　) 3. 高雄夏天的時候會下大雨，也會有颱風。

(　) 4. 高雄的秋天比夏天涼快得多。

(　) 5. 白老師跟他的姐姐已經很久沒見面了。

(　) 6. 白老師的姐姐住在美國東部的一個大城市裏。

(　) 7. 白老師想在波士頓住兩個星期。

C. This is a map of Taiwan. Underline all the Chinese characters that you can recognize and also circle the names of the cities that you have learned.

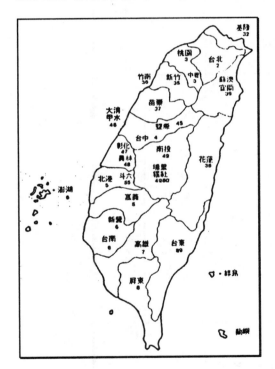

IV. Writing and Grammar Exercises

Section One

A. Following the model, complete the sentences using "以爲...呢"

Example: 今天星期五，===> 今天星期五，我以爲是星期四呢。

1. 學中文不太難，_____。

2. 他沒有健康保險，_____。

3. 你怎麼現在才來，_____。

4. 他籃球打得非常好，_____。

5. 你昨天去公園玩了嗎？_____。

B. Complete the sentences based on the picture below.

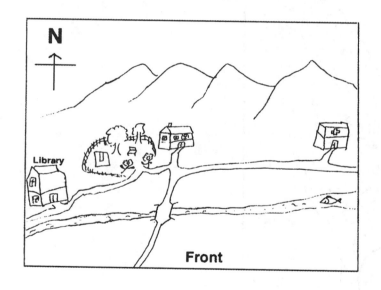

我宿舍的前面有_____，東邊是_____，

西邊是_____。宿舍的後邊有_____。

宿舍和圖書館中間是_____。

C. Following the model, rewrite the sentences below.

Example: 台北的夏天很熱，東京的夏天也很熱。

===> 台北的夏天跟東京差不多，都很熱。

1. 打籃球很有意思，打網球也很有意思。

2. 這件紅衣服很好看，那件白衣服也不難看。

3. 從宿舍到圖書館很近，到電腦中心也不遠。

4. 這家中國飯館很便宜，那家韓國飯館也不貴。

5. 從洛杉磯到台北，華航的機票是$1, 500, 西北航空公司的機票是$1, 499, 都很貴。

D. Complete the sentences based on the picture on next page.

我房間的牆上掛_____。

床的旁邊放 _____。

書桌的左邊 _____ 衣櫃。

衣櫃 _____衣服。

E. Give the Chinese equivalents to the following terms for relatives.

1. grandpa & grandma (on father's side) :

2. grandpa & grandma (on mother's side) :

3. mom's brother and his wife:

4. elder brother's wife :

5. younger sister's husband:

6. granddaughter (on daughter's side) :

F. Complete the following sentences with 比方說.

1. 我的家鄉一年四季都很好，_____。

2. 他的親戚很多，_____。

3. 我春假有很多計劃，_____。

4. 加州什麼都有，_____。

5. 麻州的風景很好，_____。

G. Answer the following questions using adj./V + 是 + adj./V, 可是/ 但是 .

　　　Example: *A:* 那件襯衫好看嗎？

　　　　　　　　B: 那件襯衫好看是好看，可是太貴了。

1. *A:* 日本飯好吃嗎？

　　B: _____ 。

2. *A:* 滑雪有意思嗎？

　　B: _____

3. *A:* 你喜歡打籃球嗎？

　　B: _____

4. *A:* 你租的公寓便宜嗎？

　　B: _____

H. Translate the following into Chinese.

1. I thought he was dead. (以為)

2. Behind the store is the computer center. (existence)

3. Your hometown doesn't sound bad at all. (聽起來)

4. I can write almost all the characters from Lesson One to Lesson Ten.
    (topic-comment, 差不多)

5. There is a very good restaurant across the street from the university.

6. I plan to go to the mountains to ski during the spring break.

7. Li You has been to many places such as Massachusetts, California, Beijing, and so on.
    (比方說)

8. She likes to read with the TV on. (開著)

9. I don't like to eat while standing up.

10. She lives in the countryside. There is a river near her house. Many trees were planted along the river. In spring, the flowers bloom abundantly in the trees. （著）

11. The beef in that restaurant is delicious, but very expensive. (Adj./V 是 Adj./V)

12. I thought that your aunt was a tour guide.

13. He wrote his name on my dictionary.

14. My uncle is working in San Francisco.

15. It sounds like California's scenery is extremely beautiful.

Section Two

A. Write a paragraph to describe the environment and climate of your hometown.

B. Write a paragraph to introduce your family members, including what they do and where they live.

Lesson Twenty-Three   At the Airport

I. Listening Comprehension

Section One (Listen to the tape for the textbook)

A. Dialogue I (True/False)

(   ) 1. Li You helped Wang Peng pack.
(   ) 2. Wang Peng drove to the airport by himself.
(   ) 3. The airport parking lot was completely full.
(   ) 4. The man's luggage was overweight.
(   ) 5. The man has no carry-on luggage.
(   ) 6. The woman cried because she did not want to leave her parents.
(   ) 7. The man will be back after a month.
(   ) 8. The woman asked the man to call her.
(   ) 9. The man promised the woman that he would drive carefully.
(   ) 10. The woman wished the man a nice trip.

B. Dialogue II (True/False)

(   ) 1. Wang Peng's cousin came to the airport to meet him because Wang Peng's parents could not come.
(   ) 2. Wang Peng's cousin is younger than him.
(   ) 3. Wang Peng has lost some weight.
(   ) 4. Wang Peng was on the airplane for more than 20 hours.
(   ) 5. Wang Peng's grandparents passed away a few years ago.
(   ) 6. They will go home in Wang Peng's cousin's car.

Section Two (Listen to the tape for the workbook)

A. Narrative (Multiple choice)

(   ) 1. How many years has Little Gao's aunt lived in Los Angeles?
     a. More than ten years.
     b. Almost ten years.
     c. Twenty years.
     d. Ten months.

(   ) 2. Where did she and her friends have dinner yesterday afternoon?
     a. At a restaurant in Boston.
     b. At one of her friends' house.
     c. At a Chinese restaurant in Los Angeles.
     d. At her own house.

(   ) 3. Her furniture was _____ last week.
     a. sold   b. shipped
     c. given to friends   d. rented out
(   ) 4. Today she is taking _____ to the airport.

129

a. three suitcases full of clothes
b. three suitcases and some gifts
c. three suitcases of gifts from her friends in Los Angeles
d. three suitcases of gifts for her friends in Boston

(   ) 5. At the airport, Little Gao's aunt _____.
a. bid farewell to her friends repeatedly
b. talked for a long time to her friends but forgot to say good-bye
c. was too emotional to say anything
d. wanted to remain silent because she spoke too much yesterday

(   ) 6. Which of the following statements best reflects Little Gao's aunt's feelings as she prepares to leave?
a. Little Gao's aunt realizes that Los Angeles is a much better city than she thought.
b. Little Gao's aunt feels it is very hard to leave her friends.
c. Little Gao's aunt realizes that she will miss the Chinese restaurants in Los Angeles.
d. Little Gao's aunt feels very sad to be traveling alone.

B. Dialogue (Multiple choice)
(   ) 1. The dialogue is most likely to have taken place _____.
a. at the Chicago airport
b. on the airplane
c. at the Boston airport
d. at the Los Angeles airport

(   ) 2. Approximately how many hours did the trip take altogether?
a. three   b. four and half   c. six   d. seven

(   ) 3. What was the weather probably like when the dialogue was taking place? It was _____.
a. sunny but cold
b. cold and rainy
c. snowy
d. windy and rainy

(   ) 4. How did the woman feel on her arrival? She felt _____.
a. cold but not hungry
b. both cold and hungry
c. neither cold nor hungry
d. hungry but not cold

II. Speaking Exercises

Section One (Answer the questions in Chinese based on the dialogues)

A. Dialogue I

1. What does Wang Peng intend to do during the summer vacation?
2. What did Li You remind Wang Peng to do when Wang Peng was about to go on a journey?
3. Did they find a parking space at the airport? Please explain.
4. What did the woman ask the man? How did the man reply?
5. What did the woman say to the man after checking in his luggage?
6. What did the man say to the woman when he found out why she was crying?
7. What did the man promise the woman to do after returning to his country?
8. What did the woman ask the man to do?
9. What did the man say to the woman before he boarded the plane?
10. What did the woman say to the man before he boarded the plane?

B. Dialogue II
1. What did Wang Peng's cousin say to him when he saw Wang Peng? How did Wang Peng reply?
2. What did the woman say to Wang Peng? How did Wang Peng reply?
3. How did Wang Peng reply when the woman said that Wang Peng must be awfully tired?
4. Who is waiting for them at home? Why?

Section Two

A. The semester is over now; you are in the airport seeing your best friend off. Your friend is kind of sad. You promise that you will call him/her. He/she hopes that you can visit him/her when you have time.

B. Find one or two classmates to role play the following situation. You just got off the airplane. Your family members have come to meet you at the airport. It has been two years since you last saw your family. You want to know how everybody is doing. They want to know if you are tired from the long trip and what your life abroad was like.

C. How do you say "Have a nice trip!" in Chinese?

D. How do you say "Take care of yourself." in Chinese?

III. Reading Exercises

Section One

A. Dialogue I

1. 王朋爲什麽要回中國？

2. 他是怎麽到機場的？

3. 爲什麽李友花了很久時間才找到一個停車位？

4. 王朋坐哪家航空公司的飛機？

5. 王朋有幾件行李要托運？

6. 上飛機的時候要什麽東西？

7. 王朋在什麽地方上飛機？

8. 王朋和李友現在在機場的什麽地方？

9. 你想李友爲什麽哭了？

10. 李友要王朋打電話給她嗎？ 爲什麽？

11. 送人的時候，可以說什麼客氣的話？

B. Dialogue II

1. 哪些人到機場來接王朋？

2. 誰要幫王朋拿行李？

3. 為什麼王朋瘦了五公斤？

4. 王朋坐了多長時間的飛機才到北京？

5. 王朋家裏還有哪些人？

6. 王朋的父母開車來接王朋嗎？你是怎麼知道的？

Section Two

A. Read the passage and answer the questions. (True/False)

> 　　小張第一次來美國讀書的時候，他的爸爸、媽媽和妹妹都到機場去送他。因為小張的行李太多了，他們家的汽車放不下，所以爸爸跟媽媽開家裏的車，小張跟妹妹是坐出租汽車到機場去的。因為這是小張第一次出國，他的爸媽都很擔心，一直跟他説到美國以後應該注意的事。要上飛機的時候，小張的媽媽流了眼淚，妹妹也哭了。小張的爸爸要小張一到美國就打電話回家，告訴他們他到美國了。

(　) 1. 小張出國的時候，他的父母和妹妹都到機場去送他。

(　) 2. 小張跟妹妹開車去機場。

(　) 3. 小張來美國以前沒有出過國。

(　) 4. 小張來美國讀書，他的父母一點都不擔心。

(　) 5. 小張要上飛機的時候，他的媽媽、妹妹都哭了。

B. Read the passage and answer the questions. (True/False)

> 　　今天小白的父母和哥哥到高雄機場去接她。小白到美國念了兩年書，現在她從研究所畢業了。小白一直沒有回過家，所以家裏的人都很想念她。飛機應該晚上十點三刻到高雄機場，可是在台北轉機的時候，因為天氣不好，飛機晚了一個半小時。飛機到了以後，小白又等了差不多半個多小時才等到她托運的兩件行李。雖然小白的爸爸媽媽等了兩個多小時，有點累了，可是他們一看到了小白就一點都不覺得累了。

(　) 1. 小白是在美國讀研究所的。

(　) 2. 小白等到研究所畢業以後才回台灣。

(　) 3. 小白的飛機從美國直飛高雄。

(　) 4. 小白的行李都是自己隨身帶著，沒有托運。

(　) 5. 小白見到她的家人的時候應該差不多半夜一點鐘了。

IV. Writing and Grammar Exercises

Section One

A. Complete the following short conversations with 就行了.

1. *A:* 我下個月就要去中國了，你有什麼事情嗎？（寫信）

    B: _____ 。

2. 學生：明天的考試，我們應該怎麼復習？（最後三課）

    老師：_____ 。

3. *A:* 到學校圖書館怎麼走？（往右拐，一直往前走）

    B: _____ 。

4. *A:* 我最近越來越瘦了，怎麼辦？（多吃飯）

    B: _____ 。

5. *A:* 我住的房間很舒服，可是太貴。我不知道怎麼辦。（找朋友一起住）

    B: _____ 。

B. Fill in the blanks with "才"、"還"

    我的妹妹很小，上個月_____兩歲。這個月我回家的時候見到她，沒想到
_____過了一個月她已經會說很多話了。她不但會說幾句英文，_____會說一
點中文，而且她的發音_____不錯。

C. Complete the following sentences using "好像".

1. 他一直流眼淚，也不說話，＿＿＿＿＿＿＿＿＿＿＿＿＿＿＿＿＿＿＿＿＿＿＿＿。
   (sad)

2. 他家裏的書多極了，＿＿＿＿＿＿＿＿＿＿＿＿＿＿＿＿＿＿＿＿＿＿＿＿＿。
   (library)

3. 他開車開得很好，＿＿＿＿＿＿＿＿＿＿＿＿＿＿＿＿＿＿＿＿＿＿＿＿＿＿。
   (drive for a long time)

4. 回到房間以後她一直不說話，＿＿＿＿＿＿＿＿＿＿＿＿＿＿＿＿＿＿＿＿。
   (unhappy)

5. 他見了我不說話，＿＿＿＿＿＿＿＿＿＿＿＿＿＿＿＿＿＿＿＿＿＿＿＿＿＿。
   (do not know me)

D. Fill in the blanks using "的，得 or 地"

我＿＿＿＿朋友去中國已經一年了。昨天他回來了。我高興＿＿＿＿去飛機場接他。一年沒見，他好像長＿＿＿＿更高了。他送給我＿＿＿＿禮物是一本中文書，可是我＿＿＿＿中文學＿＿＿＿不太好，所以看不懂。因為我們很久沒在一起了，所以昨天晚上我們去一家很貴＿＿＿＿飯館好好＿＿＿＿慶祝了一下。

E. Translate the following into Chinese.

1. The parking lot is filled with cars. We almost failed to find a parking space. (差一點)

2. I will write to you as soon as I get to New York. Take good care of yourself.
    (多保重)

3. I don't want to buy another computer. This one will do just fine. (就行了)

4. My mother used to say, "Don't talk while you eat. It's a bad habit." (一邊...一邊)

5. After I learned who he was, I almost let out a cry. (...以後，差一點)

6. He seems as though he doesn't want to go to the opera with Li You. (好像)

7. The food in this Japanese restaurant is not bad. (還)

8. Wang Peng is only two years older than Li You. (才)

9. Grandmother (maternal) doesn't have the strength to carry her luggage. Hurry up and
    help her carry the luggage.   (V + potential complement)

10. My brother's desk is very small. (的，地，得)

11. He walks very fast, but runs pretty slow. (的，地，得)

12. After eating her lunch quickly, she went to her class. (的，地，得)

13. I was not accustomed to eating American food, so I lost 10 kilograms. (V + potential complement)

14. The airplane is about to take off! Please take good care of yourself. Bon voyage.

Section Two

A. Write a letter to your friends in Chinese. Tell them that you are going to China to see them, ask them to pick you up at the airport, and give them your flight information.

B. Write a paragraph describing your experience of flying. Be sure to mention the food and the seat.